GIVING FLIGHT TO
IMAGINATION

LEADERSHIP, IMAGINATION, AND EXCELLENCE

GIVING FLIGHT TO
IMAGINATION

LEADERSHIP, IMAGINATION, AND EXCELLENCE

DR. JOSÉ V. "ZITO" SARTARELLI, PhD
WITH DALENE BICKEL

Copyright © 2023 by Giving Flight to Imagination, LLC

All rights reserved. No part of this book may be reproduced in any form or by any means electronic or mechanical, including but not limited to photocopying, recording, or any information storage and retrieval system, without permission in writing from the author.

Although the publisher and the authors have made every effort to ensure the information in this book was correct at the time of printing and while this publication is designed to provide accurate information in regard to the subject matter covered, the publisher and the authors assume no responsibility for errors, inaccuracies, omissions, or any other inconsistencies herein and hereby disclaim any liability to any party for any loss, damage, or disruption caused by errors or omissions, whether such errors or omissions result from negligence, accident, or any other cause.

Cover and interior design by G Sharp Design, LLC
Cover Photo by Jeff Janowski

ISBN 979-8-218-30467-6 (paperback)
ISBN 979-8-218-30468-3 (hardcover)
ISBN 979-8-218-30469-0 (ebook)

To everyone who has helped give flight
to my imagination, particularly my wife,
Katherine Ann "Kathy" Sartarelli.

CONTENTS

Preface ix
Acknowledgments... xi
Chapter 1   Tomatoes to the Rescue 1
Chapter 2   AFS Changed My Life............................... 21
Chapter 3   Triumph Through Scholarships 41
Chapter 4   Fighting the Good Fight 61
Chapter 5   The Arena Goes Global 93
Chapter 6   Doing Well by Doing Good......................... 127
Chapter 7   The Academy at Last 153
Chapter 8   Imagination at Its Best 221
Chapter 9   Reflections and Observations 227
Chapter 10   Mentors 237
Epilogue 259
Family Tree.. 264
About the Author... 271

PREFACE

Why an autobiography? Once I retired from the position of chancellor of the University of North Carolina Wilmington and looked back on my career and life and the journey it has taken me on, from a small farm in Brazil to a successful career in international business and academia, I thought there might be an interesting story in this progression.

The beginning was in another time and world altogether. A bronchitis-prone little boy living on a rural farm in the interior of Brazil in the 1950s, through chance and hard work, but more than that, through the kindness and character of the people who surrounded him, is allowed to study and work his way up to enter the world of academia, ultimately becoming chancellor of one of the top one hundred public universities in the United States. This after thirty years of a successful career working for three of the most respected pharmaceutical companies in the world, where improving and saving lives is the paramount goal.

As I thought more about it, I realized that leadership, imagination, and excellence were the elements that translated into the successes in my life. And underpinning it all was education.

Education always came first. My desire to study was the impetus that drove me to seek out the highest level of education, a PhD.

With that in mind, I sought to write a book that wouldn't just serve as a legacy of my accomplishments, but one that would also offer valuable insights and encourage you to give flight to your own imagination. I was fortunate to find a talented "partner in crime" in Dalene Bickel, who has collected all my intellectual meanderings, interviewed me extensively, and put together this autobiography that I hope you will enjoy reading.

José Valentim Sartarelli
September 2023

ACKNOWLEDGMENTS

Many people contributed to the making of this autobiography.

I would like to thank my sister, Luzia Sartarelli Joaquim, for all her insights and fact-checking; my oldest brother Aristeu Sartarelli; and my uncle, Gilberto Sartarelli. In addition, I would like to recognize my best friend, José Sergio Laureano, for his insights on the overall story, as well as Valentina Menghi, another classmate from the early days who has remained a close friend. My profound thanks also go to my sister-in-law, Susan Strong, and her husband, John Stillian, for their insights.

At the beginning of my career in Indianapolis, Vern Altmeyer and Don Joyce were incredible supporters. I am indebted to the professional and loyal Lilly executives, particularly those in Chile and Brazil, who shared in both my accomplishments and challenges, and in Singapore, who made trips with me out of Changi Airport time and time again as a team.

I have benefitted from profound discussions with each of my former bosses and friends, Roy Cage and Christine Poon. The cooperation, travel, and accomplishments we shared at Eli Lilly, BMS, and Johnson & Johnson were always enjoyable and are an integral part of this autobiography.

Special thanks go to all the students, faculty, staff, alumni, and donors at WVU and UNCW who, for twelve years, helped shape my experiences in the academy. In addition, a heartfelt thank-you to all my assistants in both business and academia who made my success possible.

I would like to thank the other chancellors of the University of North Carolina system who were my companions in dealing with natural disasters, the coronavirus pandemic, and divisive politics and in acting as a protective shield around their students and their universities to accomplish the important goals of educating, inspiring, and rewarding students at every stage of their college career.

Finally, my wife, Kathy, has provided context to significant parts of the story. She has edited every chapter and added information that may have been missing, and she has typed pages and pages of my basic text, which she then passed along to my co-author to incorporate into the manuscript.

While many have contributed to make this book better, I take full responsibility for its faults.

Thank you, thank you, thank you.

1

TOMATOES TO THE RESCUE

There's a popular phrase that says "Home is where our story begins." Such is the case for me, José Valentim "Zito" Sartarelli. My story begins in 1940s Brazil in Sitio Boa Vista dos Freitas,[1] a three-hour drive from the state capital of São Paulo.[2]

Back then, approximately 50 percent of Brazil's population lived in similar rural farming areas. It was not unusual to see large farms (*fazendas*) containing multiple homes (*colonias*) and accompanying vegetable gardens for the workers and their families. This was how my grandfather Rosario Sartarelli and his family lived until 1944, when he transitioned from being a colonia worker to a farm owner.

When Grandfather learned that the nearby Freitas family *sitio* (small farm) was for sale, he invited his eldest son, Joáo (my father), to partner with him to purchase the approximately one-hundred-acre

[1] A municipality of Ribeirão Bonito, approximately five miles from the town of Ribeirão Bonito (Beautiful Creek).
[2] São Paulo continues to be the largest state in the country (currently home to about forty-five million people) and the most successful, generating about a third of the entire GDP. This is particularly notable since Brazil is a large country, about the same size as the United States, including Alaska and Hawaii.

property.[3] Never would they have imagined that just a few months after entering into a gentleman's agreement[4] to buy the sitio together, my grandfather would unexpectedly die, thereby leaving all one hundred acres to his wife, Maria Fontati.

Father continued to honor their agreement by overseeing the sitio's daily operations, raising such cash crops as corn, manioc,[5] cotton, rice, and coffee. In addition, at harvesttime, he retained only what our family needed for our own consumption and then transferred a third of the receipts of the cotton crops to his mother and siblings before selling the surplus for a profit.

When they purchased the sitio, it boasted only one brick house on the western side of the property, which was claimed by my grandparents and their ten other living children.[6] A mud house (*casa de barro*) was quickly erected a half mile away on the eastern side for my father, mother, and their four children: Aristeu "Tilim," João Carlos "Carlito," Maria Aparecida "Cidinha," and Isaura. Luzia joined the family in 1947 and I arrived in 1949.[7] All six of us—three boys and three girls—were born at home with the assistance of Grandmother Sartarelli, who was an experienced midwife.

The mud house was primitive but served its purpose by protecting us from the elements. The exterior consisted of wood-framed walls covered by hardened red clay and a ceramic-tile roof. The interior contained three bedrooms, a kitchen, a living room, and one storage room.

---

3 The equivalent of sixteen *alqueires paulistas*.
4 An undocumented, thereby unofficial, agreement.
5 A tuber, also commonly known as cassava or yucca, that is frequently sliced and fried.
6 Three other children had died at young ages.
7 By the time I was born, Tilim was fourteen, Carlito was eleven, Cidinha was nine, Isaura was seven, and Luzia was two.

An artist's rendering of our mud house as it appeared in the late 1940s/early 1950s, Sitio Boa Vista dos Freitas, Ribeirão Bonito, S.P., Brazil. The home was eventually demolished and, unfortunately, no photo of it was ever kept.

We did not have electricity, which meant no running water or even a radio. Therefore, we remained relatively unaware of the destruction and horrors taking place in the rest of the world during World War II. In fact, very few Brazilians were impacted by the war since only a small contingent of Força Expedicionária Brasileira (FEB) partnered with American forces in Italy for less than a year.[8]

During the war, U.S. President FDR talked a lot about the United States being the arsenal of democracy and the importance of maintaining friendships with Latin American countries to prevent them from supporting the Germans, who had a strong presence there at that time. Since Brazil was more pro-U.S than its neighbors, they sent men to participate in the war—the only country in Latin America to do so. In return, the U.S. later helped Brazil develop economically.

---

8 The Força Expedicionária Brasileira consisted of mostly professional soldiers who were already conscripted and serving at that time. They served under U.S. General Clark and engaged in many battles, including the successful Allied advance at Monte Castello.

Thus sheltered from the outside world, my siblings and I enjoyed a happy, productive home life. Our mother, Dona Alzira,[9] like my father, had received only a limited formal education, but she didn't let that—or the eventual blindness in her left eye—prevent her from successfully raising six children and managing the house. She made her own household products from natural ingredients, churned her own butter, cooked on a woodstove, and maintained an immaculately clean home. She also made our clothes and, later in life, made extra money as a seamstress, altering and repairing clothes for people in town.

Mother was a lady with strong religious convictions and demonstrated a natural resilience to difficulties. She was creative and an out-of-the-box, flight-to-imagination type of person whereas my father was much more circumspect. But both were honest and hardworking.

Mother's family, the Ramos dos Santos, was six in all and also lived on farms around Ribeirão Bonito. Her mother, Luciana, was of Portuguese stock and died before her husband, Benedito, who eventually became ill and moved in with our family for a few months before he passed away in 1944.

Left: Alzira Ramos Dos Santos Sartarelli in her sixties or early seventies.
Right: Joáo "Rosario" Sartarelli in his thirties or forties.

9 She was called "Dona Alzira" by everyone except her husband, children, and closest friends. "Dona" is a Brazilian honorific title for every woman, similar to "Ms." in the United States.

From the day I was born unil the age of five-and-a-half, I was plagued with bronchitis. Fearing that physical punishment might worsen my condition, Father made it clear to my mother and all my siblings that they should never spank me. So even though they were occasionally upset with my behavior, they didn't dare lay a hand on me. It made for a happy early childhood.

I learned the alphabet from my eldest sister, Cidinha,[10] and when I turned seven, I joined Luzia at the small Francelim farm school one mile west of our property. Luzia and I loved going to school, walking there together in the morning and returning home for lunch. Unfortunately, our formal education ended a year-and-a-half later when the local government closed all the rural schools to ensure higher-quality education in the towns. Without transportation and the funds to pay for the required school uniforms and supplies, this left Luzia and me, and all the other farm children in the area, with spare time on our hands.

My sister Cidinha on her wedding day with her husband, Clemente Gomez.

After completing our daily chores, Luzia and I pursued individual activities of our own liking; I particularly enjoyed building miniature houses and bridges out of clay. I quickly developed a suntan

---

10 At the age of eighteen, Cidinha married Clemente Gomez, a handsome fellow from the *Grama* sitio, and they moved to his sitio.

from being outdoors so much, playing with my terrier, Gulo, and like most Brazilian boys, playing soccer (*futebol*). We didn't have formal teams or goal nets; we simply played "pickup" games in whatever fields weren't being used for crops.

Soccer was the only national sport back then. Today there's volleyball and surfing and car racing, but back in those days, there was soccer, soccer, and more soccer. Not surprisingly, all that emphasis on one sport paid off. Brazil is currently the only country in the world to have won five FIFA World Cups (Germany and Italy each have four), which made it a favored contender for the 2022 World Cup in Qatar. Sadly, Brazil did not bring home a sixth trophy that year.

The sport even played a part in my nickname. While "Zito" is diminutive for my given name (José), mother first began to refer to me as Zito, I believe, because there was a soccer player named Zito when Brazil won the World Cup in both 1958 and 1962.

Despite our relative freedom to do as we pleased, Luzia and I yearned to go back to school. We used to daydream about moving to town, wearing school uniforms, and developing great relationships with our instructors and classmates.

A photo of me as a young boy in town.

Our family never lacked food or clothing or main staples, but we didn't have much left over for discretionary spending. That's why, at Christmastime, I looked forward to riding to town with father and my siblings in our horse-drawn buggy (*charrete*) to make our once-a-year purchase of two crates of Guaraná—a popular Brazilian soft drink. Since we didn't have a refrigerator at home in which to chill the soda bottles, we placed them in the cold streams on our property—crates and all.

I grew up in a time of deep religiosity in Brazil. Every summer, our family celebrated *Festas Juninhas* (June Festivals) to honor the days of Saint Anthony (June 13), Saint John (June 24), and Saint Peter (June 29). These *Juninhas* parties were popular throughout Brazil (second only to Carnival) and always involved a lot of food, *quentao*,[11] and the raising of a mast to Saints Anthony, John, and Peter. They're still celebrated in some areas of Brazil today but are not as widespread as they once were.

The mast to the three saints on our sitio.

---

[11] A traditional Brazilian drink made up of ginger, red apples, sugar, cloves, cinnamon, and *cachaça* (sugarcane rum).

My family also regularly joined thousands of other Brazilians to make pilgrimages to cathedrals of reputation such as the Sanctuary of Our Lady of Tambau, which was about 100 kilometers (60 miles) from Ribeirão Bonito, and Aparecida do Norte, which was approximately 400 kilometers (roughly 250 miles) from our sitio. The Sanctuary of Our Lady of Aparecida is today the second-largest Catholic church in the world and the most visited sanctuary in Latin America, receiving more than seven million visitors per year.

There isn't a major pilgrimage destination in the U.S., but if you go to France, they have Lourdes and if you go to Portugal, they have Fatima; there are many in Spain and Italy, and in Brazil, there's the Sanctuary of Our Lady of Aparecida, which is our country's patron saint. This is the sanctuary that my family visited most often.

I made my first pilgrimage with my family around the age of seven. Unlike our European counterparts who traditionally hike for days to complete their pilgrimages, we Brazilians tended to drive to the destinations. Upon our arrival, we joined the long lines to enter the sanctuaries where we thanked our saint for a grace received or asked for an intercession.

ELECTRICITY & THE RISE OF "PIAUí E PERIGOSO"

The 1950s was a monumental decade for my family. By the time I turned six, my parents had enough money to construct a wood house (*casa de tabua*) at a higher elevation to protect against flooding and installed solid floors instead of the traditional hard clay. It was a comfortable house. Father also built a chapel for Mother's prayer time, corrals for the horses and milking cows, and a pigsty. Our hens were allowed to roam freely.

By the middle of the decade, electricity arrived at the sitio thanks to the initiative of Laercio Pessa,[12] a neighbor who dammed the creek that crossed his farm and ours. He then installed turbines and a generator large enough to electrify not only our farms but others throughout the valley as well. Each family had to provide their own wires and posts, but no one had to pay to use the electricity.

Lightbulbs, to me, were the most drastic and welcome change. When I had attended school, I had to study at night by the kerosene lamp, which wasn't very bright and always created shadows, making it difficult to position myself so I could read my books and write clearly. But with electricity, I was able to easily read long into the evening and our family could listen to music, the news, and even dramaturgy on the radio. A television never entered our home.

Wood house in the mid-1950s. The wooden house was demolished in the 1980s by my uncle José "Ze," who had bought out the other heirs and consolidated the property in his name. Note the electric wires that began providing power from the municipality in the 1970s/1980s, thereby replacing our neighbor's generator. Sitio Boa Vista dos Freitas, Ribeirão Bonito, S.P., Brazil.

---

12 Later, Laercio's brother, Ayrton Pessa, married my father's sister, Aparecida.

Ribeirão Bonito, the town where our sitio was located, did not have its own radio station, but the nearby town of Brotas had a station that played country (*sertaneja*) music. Soon, my brothers Tilim and Carlito began playing guitars and singing *sertaneja* music for family and friends. Carlito became very good at writing song lyrics while Tilim crafted the melodies. They named themselves Piauí e Perigoso[13] and eventually, they were invited to perform at events in Brotas. They acquired a following and competed in an all-around country music competition—and won. They were so good that they were even invited to develop a demo record.

Piauí e Perigoso (Tilim to the left and Carlito in the center) playing *sertaneja* music for their fans.

While on their travels, Tilim and Carlito began to learn about an increasingly popular experimental crop: tomatoes. The rumor was that if you could raise a large quantity of tomatoes, you could make a lot of money. Excited by the possibility, my brothers, at the ages of twenty-two and nineteen, convinced our father to dedicate a portion of the sitio to raising tomatoes. Father, in turn, asked them to make a difficult decision.

13 "Piauí" is the name of a Brazilian state and "perigoso" means "reckless."

Everyone close to Tilim and Carlito was excited about their blossoming music career. However, Father was concerned about the conflicts that would arise if they continued to pursue their artistic activities in tandem with the new tomato endeavor.

Thus, my brothers made the difficult decision to give up country singing and remain on the sitio. I strongly believe they were distraught by this, but they were resilient and willing to subjugate their artistic future for the benefit of the family as a whole.

TOMATOES TO THE RESCUE

The new crop required a monumental change for my family, who had spent many years cultivating traditional crops such as corn, cotton, rice, and coffee. Father assumed great risk by experimenting with an unfamiliar crop, particularly one that was susceptible to frost.

Carlito and Tilim located someone with experience to help us get started and the first seedlings went in the ground in the summer of 1957. As the tomatoes grew, we staked them—a process that was just horrible on one's legs and back. But once the tomatoes were staked and growing vertically, harvesting became easier because they could be plucked from the vines at arm height rather than bending over to pick them up off the ground.

In the end, the gamble paid off. Through diligence, hard work, and a prime location, the inaugural tomato crop of 1958 was a great success. Not only did the elements combine to bring about healthy plants and wonderful fruit, but the microclimate of our sitio also did not suffer the frost that affected the rest of the state of São Paulo that season.

We sold our first harvest of tomatoes at small, traditional grocery stores (the first large supermarket in Brazil didn't open until about

1960) and farm markets in the surrounding towns and cities. With limited competition in the market that year, the prices spiked, netting us an amount of cash previously unheard of by my family. With a portion of the proceeds, Father purchased our family's first vehicle—a 1932 Ford pickup truck.

FAMILY FEUD

News spread quickly about our good fortune. The next season, my uncles decided to plant tomatoes, too, and suddenly, tomatoes were "happening" throughout the sitio.

One beautiful afternoon, I was outside playing when my father returned from spraying the fields with insecticide. A few moments later, a car pulled up in front of him and I was surprised to discover that the driver was Uncle Tito. Tito had left the farm fourteen years prior to make his way in the city of São Carlos and had done well for himself by owning and operating a taxicab.

Soon, I overheard harsh words being exchanged between the two of them and watched in shock as Tito pushed Father to the ground. Mother ran out of the house carrying a stick, which she used to hit Tito until he got off Father, who was weighed down by the sprayer on his back. Tito returned to his car and drove to Grandmother's house.

Father explained that Tito had come to demand that a third of the tomato profits be given to the family in addition to the third of the cotton crops. Father considered that to be absurd since the tomatoes had not been part of the original agreement with their father and because he had religiously upheld his end of the bargain, giving the due contribution of the cotton to the family without fail.

Father's refusal infuriated Tito. Later that same day, my grandmother came to our home. She stated that indeed, a third of the tomato harvest was due her from that moment forward. Furthermore, she indicated that if the extra money was not forthcoming, Father should leave the sitio altogether.

It is unknown why she decided to take the side of Tito and break away from the agreement that had been in effect between my father and grandfather for more than a decade, but Father rejected both demands.

The ensuing days, weeks, and months were stressful and unpleasant. Even though Tito had returned to São Carlos, divisiveness remained among the other family members, all of whom sided with Tito. Everyone took great pains to avoid us and we them. My older brothers and mother wanted to leave the farm and move to town, but Father was a man of his word and was adamant that he would continue to honor the agreement he had made with his father.

In the end, my parents compromised: our family moved to town, but Father returned to the sitio every day to care for his portion of the fields. Father and Uncle Tito never spoke to each other again and went to their graves without reconciling.

As unfortunate as the situation was, it's a part of human nature. If there aren't some relatives that don't get along, it's not a real family.

THE MOVE TO TOWN

In January 1959, we moved from the wood house on the sitio into a rented home in the small town of Ribeirão Bonito. Carlito bought a store that was part grocery, part convenience store, and part bar. He sold all kinds of things: sandwiches, beverages, liquor (anyone could buy it regardless of age), and vegetables and fruits, including, of course, our tomatoes.

Tilim took a job with a local sugar mill. Brazil remains the largest producer of sugar in the world today; if you go to the state of São Paulo, you'll see sugarcane everywhere. Tilim contracted workers in town and transported them to the sugar mill's fields and back. Nowadays, sugarcane is cut by machines, but back then it was all cut by hand. There were a lot of laborers to be transported.

Since Father never learned to drive the truck he bought, he made the approximately five-mile daily commute to the farm in his *charrete*. He downsized his crops to only what he could manage by himself yet would bring in enough money to pay for our expenses. A year or so later, he had saved up enough money to buy a house in town, moving us out of our rental.

Mother maintained the house, watched over her family, and helped at Carlito's store. My sister Isaura continued to live with us and worked as a seamstress. As for Luzia and me, we finally got to go back to school.

We were grateful to attend the state-run school but, of course, we faced some adjustments and challenges as well. For example, I, like many other former farm boys, was bestowed the nickname "hillbilly," which I tried to ignore as I focused on my studies. It worked. Luzia and I became the top students from day one because we loved school and we felt that if we were going to attend school, we wanted to be the best.

I've always worked toward excellence in whatever I do. My goal has always been to become an accomplished person; if I'm going to do something, I want to do it well. When I saw people doing certain things that I wanted to do, I realized I *could* do it with the right training. Everything is in the realm of possibilities through education. So I determined to get all the education I could so that people could never rule me out for a position because of a lack of education. For me, school was the lever to advance my career and life.

But my education wasn't limited to just school. Newspapers, I discovered, contained a wealth of important information about what was happening locally, nationally, and around the world. When my brother Carlito purchased the small store in town, its existing subscription to *O Estado de São Paulo* (the *Estado*), one of the top three newspapers in Brazil, remained in place. I credit it for fostering my love for reading.

I scoured the paper from top to bottom every day, paying particular attention to its coverage of world news, which continues to pique my interest today. Kathy and I are two of the few people in our current neighborhood who still subscribe to the *New York Times,* the *Wall Street Journal,* and the *Naples Daily News.* Some subscribe to the local paper, but the rest of it they must get from the Internet.

I'm standing beside a map of Brazil in Ribeirão Bonito during one of my more recent visits home.

IMAGINATION AT ITS BEST

All the benefits of moving to town and my education were a direct result of the success of the tomato crop that first year. At the end of the day, it's all about giving flight to imagination—taking a chance on an idea that is unusual and differentiates you, your business, or your family from everyone else. For us, it was taking a chance on tomatoes and they came to our rescue. If we had continued doing what we had been doing all along, we would still be in the same place today.

The Big Picture

1940s Overview

WORLD / U.S. [14]

- Dow:[15] 150.24–200.13, +33%
- WWII lasts half a decade; its impact lasts longer
- The West and Soviet Union jostle for leadership; beginnings of Cold War
- New institutions develop: United Nations (UN), International Monetary Fund, World Bank, Bretton Woods (an international currency exchange system), welfare state, etc.
- Decolonization under way, allowing India, Pakistan, Israel, Vietnam, and China to emerge
- Major new technologies develop: computers, nuclear power, jet propulsion
- FDR—the war effort drives everything he does
- U.S. Vice President Harry Truman takes over as president after FDR unexpectedly dies in 1945; drops the bomb on Hiroshima and Nagasaki and wins the U.S. presidential election in 1948
- Economy grows fast during the war—and after
- Chuck Yeager breaks sound barrier in 1947
- George Orwell publishes *1984* in 1949

---

14 Source of historical data in this section: "1940s," Wikimedia Foundation, https://en.wikipedia.org/wiki/1940s. Last accessed September 25, 2023.

15 Source of the Dow range in this section: "Dow Jones Industrial Average," Wikimedia Foundation, https://en.wikipedia.org/wiki/Dow_Jones_Industrial_Average. Last accessed October 24, 2023.

BRAZIL

- Força Expedicionária Brasileira goes to Italy and joins U.S. soldiers during WWII
- Country comes out of Getúlio's dictatorship in 1945
- Country remains largely rural (about 50%)

1950s Overview

WORLD / U. S. [16]

- Dow:[17] 200.13–679.36, +239%
- World continues to recover from WWII; experiences significant growth of population and economy
- Cold War accelerates with the launch of the Soviet Union's Sputnik in 1957
- Space race begins between the U.S. and the Soviet Union
- Decolonization continues in Africa and Asia
- Korean and Vietnamese wars underway
- Cuba becomes Communist in 1959

BRAZIL

- Brazil gets help from the U.S. in its development aspirations such as the Usina de Volta Redonda (steel mill) and porta-aviões (aircraft carrier)
- Getúlio Vargas becomes President of Brazil (having been a dictator from 1930–1945) and commits suicide in 1954

---

16 Source of historical data in this section: "1950s," Wikimedia Foundation, https://en.wikipedia.org/wiki/1950s. Last accessed September 25, 2023.

17 Source of the Dow range in this section: "Dow Jones Industrial Average," Wikimedia Foundation, https://en.wikipedia.org/wiki/Dow_Jones_Industrial_Average. Last accessed October 24, 2023.

- Juscelino Kubitschek becomes President (1956–1961) and his slogan sticks: "Fifty years in five years"; rapid industrialization and the construction of the new capital city of Brasília begins
- Brazil loses soccer World Cup to Uruguay at Maracana Stadium in Rio de Janeiro in 1950
- Brazil wins soccer World Cup in Sweden in 1958; Pelé emerges
- Bossa Nova music, a "new style" that blends samba and jazz, becomes popular

2

AFS CHANGED MY LIFE

The political landscape of Brazil during the 1960s is best described as tumultuous and ever changing.

First, President Juscelino Kubitschek finished his term and left in 1961. Then Jânio Quadros resigned as head of state after a year and was temporarily replaced by the president of the lower chamber of the House of Representatives, Ranieri Mazzilli. He was succeeded by João Goulart, an admirer of Fidel Castro and Che Guevara. In late 1963/early 1964, gigantic demonstrations—almost a million people—protested in the streets of São Paulo and Rio, wanting to push Goulart out because he was corrupt and leading Brazil toward communism. He was ultimately exiled to Uruguay where he eventually died. On March 31, 1964, the revolution exploded and the military stayed in power until 1985.

The presidency was then filled by General Humberto de Alencar Castelo Branco, who had served alongside U.S. troops in Italy during WWII when he was a lieutenant colonel in Brazil's Força Expedicionária Brasileira. He was a good president, honest, and received a lot of support from the U.S. But then the corporate jet he was riding in crashed; it's unknown if the crash was intentional or a true accident. In any case, Artur da Costa e Silva took over as president, but after two years died from a heart attack. The country was then briefly ruled by a three-person junta before Emílio Garrastazu Médici, an army general, assumed the presidency for five years.

This long-awaited stability in leadership, along with Médici's decision to open Brazil up to the world, enabled Brazil to grow at a booming rate of 10 percent per year between 1968 and 1974. Foreign investments poured in, and the country benefited from a liberalized economy; it was a true economic miracle. Brazil needed that injection of normalcy.

Because all this happened under the military regime, I supported them throughout the 1960s. This would later change, but early in their leadership, they did a lot of good things. The change in military behavior ("they became harsher") was in response to growing civil unrest. Those who opposed the military took up arms and initiated bomb attacks, abductions (the U.S. ambassador was kidnapped), and guerilla warfare (Araguaia) in the interior of Brazil.

The 1960s were also an inebriating decade where freedom was at the very core all around the world. Americans were demonstrating at Woodstock and Berkeley; in France, they pushed Charles de Gaulle out; and in Brazil, young people began to ask for more freedom, too. But our military government was unwilling to give it, which led to many prosecutions and persecutions for speaking out.

It was a turbulent time.

ENTERTAINMENT

Despite all this political upheaval, I enjoyed my teen years. The town of Ribeirão Bonito offered an entirely new life for me. No longer was I required to stake tomato plants and care for farm animals (we now only had cats as pets); I now spent my time studying, working at the store, and familiarizing myself with my new surroundings.

I enjoyed riding my bicycle with my new friends in town (I'm on the far left).

Morro Ribeirão Bonito, circa late 1980s/early 1990s. "Morro" means "hill" in English. The church in the background is Saint Benedict; my family attended a different church in town.

One of my best friends operated the projector at the local movie theater (Cine Piratininga), so I often joined him there to watch the latest films. Some Brazilian movies were shown, but American movies dominated the big screen. I particularly enjoyed the American cowboy Western movies; my friend and I watched them all and selected our favorite stars. That's why I love the American West today; I think it's so special.

The movies started at eight o'clock, but the young men and women liked to arrive downtown by six o'clock. The boys walked in one direction around the plaza while the girls walked the other direction, exchanging love notes or glances as they passed each other until it was time for the movie to start or the club to open. It was delightful; the small towns were so much fun up to the advent of television.

Once television entered most Brazilian homes in the 1970s, fewer people went outdoors to socialize. The plazas are still there, but they've gone quiet; no one walks them anymore. In fact, my hometown no longer has a movie theater. With the advent of TV and the rise of video games, the youth who used to be highly engaged with each other now primarily keep to themselves.

But the television wasn't all bad. When TVs became widely available in Brazil in the mid to late 1960s, our family purchased a floor model and placed it in the living room. This provided me with a front-row, black-and-white view of the space race and its many launches. Ever since my family and I had witnessed *Sputnik* race through the sky in 1957 thanks to a radio announcement alerting us to the opportunity, I had been intrigued by the ability of man to enter space.

I also remained interested in world news and continued to read the newspapers to learn about what was happening elsewhere. Before our television, the newspapers were how I discovered JFK, the American president from 1961–1963. I admired how he presented himself and how he led his country, willing to try new things such as the space race and fostering relationships with Latin American countries through the Alliance for Progress.

The more I discovered about America through newspapers, movies, and television, the more I wanted to go there to experience it for myself.

I was saddened to see on the front page of *O Estado de São Paulo* that U.S. President JFK had been assassinated on November 22, 1963.

FAITH

Once we moved to town, Mother lost her private chapel, but she most certainly didn't lose her faith. Both my parents belonged to the Catholic Church, but it was Mother who made sure my siblings and I attended. If we didn't, then we had to come up with a good explanation. My first communion was held at the church in town, and we continued to make regular pilgrimages, most often to the Sanctuary of Our Lady of Aparecida.

Left: My first communion, late 1950s.
Right: Pilgrimage to the Sanctuary of Our Lady of Aparecida. My mother, Alzira, is flanked by me (left) and my best friend, Sergio (right), 1968/1969.

In addition, Mother encouraged Luzia and I to participate in the youth organization called the crusade (*cruzada infantil*). I was the president of the crusade one year, but I never wanted to be an altar boy or be too close to the priests; my best friend had been an altar boy until he had a fight with the priest and got turned off on the church.

As I got older, I recognized that the church is made up of people. People are who they are; there are great priests and there are not-so-great priests. None of them are perfect because they're not God.

THE BENEFITS OF EDUCATION

Education was important to Luzia and me because we recognized it as our way out of poverty. We were not poor in the sense of homelessness; we were self-sustaining, but there was no discretionary income available. Father always saved and saved, but the amount of saving possible from a farmer's income is not very substantial.

At Coronel Pinto Ferraz primary school, Luzia and I benefited from multiple teachers and classes such as history, Portuguese, geography, math, and science. Throughout all four years of middle school, Dr. Piraja da Silva taught me the English language, which was a requirement to graduate. It later proved to be a most valuable asset.

I enjoyed a few school years with my best friend, José Sergio Laureano, whom I met shortly after moving to town; we've remained lifelong friends. José Sergio became a successful banker, commuting back and forth every week between his home in Ribeirão Bonito and his job in São Paulo for almost thirty years. He left on Sunday night, took the three-hour bus ride to São Paulo and lived in a *pensão* (boarding house) with other people as he worked throughout the week, and then returned home to his wife and three daughters on Friday night. It was a sacrifice, but by doing that, he was able to send all three of his girls to the university; one of them, in fact, earned a PhD.

I quickly became a top student as a result of both a natural predilection for certain subjects and a willingness to put in the necessary effort. I've always been hardworking, focused, and intentional about the things I do. Because of these qualities, I often earned positions of leadership, such as a student leader with CEDEC, an educational and cultural center that sponsored events such as choir concerts and guest speakers who were successful in their various careers. And most importantly to me, I was selected as a candidate for an American Field Service (AFS) International Scholarship to study in the United States.

AMERICA BOUND

AFS originated as a humanitarian ambulance corps in France during WWI and transitioned into a global high school exchange program at the conclusion of WWII with the goal "to perpetuate international friendships in peacetime."[18] They believed that if young people lived and studied with one another, they wouldn't go to war against each other. The student program, which brought international students to America for a year of high school while residing with a host family, quickly became popular.

I didn't know all that at the time, however. I happened to learn about the program from friends who knew a young lady from a nearby town who had participated. Excited about the potential opportunity to study in the United States, I took it upon myself to apply for an AFS scholarship. After taking the required test, I had to wait several months before learning that I was accepted for the 1967/1968 school year. When I joyfully announced the good news to my parents, my father's response was not encouraging. "Over my dead body," he said. "You're not going to go." When pressed for an explanation, he replied,

---

18 "AFS History Timeline," American Field Service website, https://afs.org/archives/timeline/#afs-nav-1948. Last accessed November 7, 2023.

"You don't need to go to America. You're now living in town, you're going to school, you're a top student. You can stay here, help me, and attend college here; we'll help you go to college." Father, as I stated earlier, hated change. He was also worried about crime and drugs. I was not concerned about that at all; I've never been concerned about those things.

Disappointed, I turned to my mother, who stated, "Of course you have to go! I'm going to cry for the next twelve months, but you've got to go."

I listened to my mother.

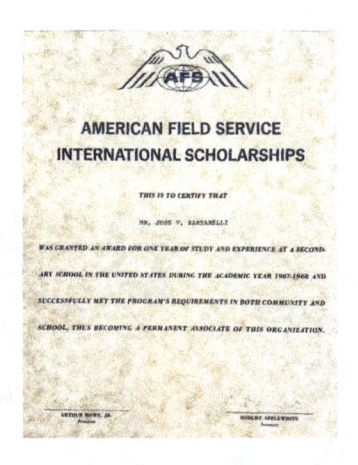

A copy of my AFS scholarship certificate.

At the time of my acceptance into the AFS program in July 1967, I was one of approximately three thousand students from sixty countries, including Thailand, Singapore, Australia, and many others throughout Europe, South America, and Africa. I flew from Rio de Janeiro, Brazil, to New York City, where I joined the other international students for orientation at Hofstra University before dispersing to our host families across the United States. I had requested to be placed in California, Texas, or Florida and was happy to learn that I was being sent to Dimmitt, Texas—a small town between Lubbock and Amarillo with a population of five thousand, which was equivalent to Ribeirão Bonito.

Despite my determination, bravado, and heartfelt belief that it was a wise decision, I also recognized that it was a risky and difficult endeavor all the same. To my father's point, it was a risk to give up on my high school education in Brazil when I was already preparing to attend college there the following year. Yet all of a sudden, I was pulling myself away from that tiny town, boarding an airplane to New York City, and going to live with strangers for a year in the second-largest state in America. It would have been a huge culture shock for any person, but it was especially so for an eighteen-year-old like me. Despite the challenges, though, I knew it was worth the risk.

Downtown Dimmitt, Texas, late 1990s.

LIFE IN THE LONE STAR STATE

My host family, Lonnie and Janice Bell and their four children, was waiting for me at the airport in Amarillo, Texas when I arrived. We exchanged greetings, but they quickly realized I could not understand anything they were saying to me. My English classes had taught me to write proficiently, but I could not speak it well and reading in English proved to be a bit of a challenge in certain situations.

The Bell family warmly welcomed me into their home for the 1967/1968 school year.
L–R: Rick, Mike, me, Jeff, Lori, Janice, and Lonnie.

For example, since it was late afternoon when I arrived, they took me to a restaurant for an early dinner, but I could not read the menu very well. The only thing I could pronounce was "salad," so I ordered a Texan salad. Then I wondered, *What's in it?* As it was placed before me, I saw it had all kinds of vegetables sitting on top of a very large bed of greens. I hated greens, but I did not want to offend my hosts, so I forced myself to eat it.

This was the beginning of many meal discoveries that required give-and-take between Janice and me. The family typically ate lots of meat and potatoes whereas I had been raised on rice and spaghetti. Janice graciously learned how to fix some of my favorite dishes for me.

Our differing religions also required a bit of compromise. Lonnie and Janice were members of the local Church of Christ, which, I quickly discovered, was fundamentalist. I attended church with them on Wednesdays and Saturdays, and on Sundays, I went to mass at the Catholic Church in the neighboring town of Nazareth. The good-hearted Ms. Bellinghausen, a resident of Dimmitt, went to the trouble of taking me to church for a full year.

The Bells were a wonderful family and I soon settled in with them. Acclimating to my new school was an equally wonderful experience. Before long, I was learning English, picking up American ways, and making great friends, some of whom I still consider friends today. My crowning achievement—literally—was when my classmates selected me as the Flame King alongside a lady classmate who was selected as the Flame Queen.

It was an honor to be awarded the title of Flame King of my senior class. Dimmitt, Texas, spring 1968.

In addition to my classroom instruction, I also spent time learning how to be a public speaker. In January 1968, I began speaking about my AFS experience at Lions Club meetings and various high schools, which I discovered was a lot of fun. I was also interviewed extensively by the *Castro County News* throughout my time in Dimmitt.

I graduated in 1968 in a class of ninety-two students. In 2018, Kathy and I attended the fiftieth class reunion in the pretty hill country of Fredericksburg, Texas, outside Austin. About twenty-five classmates had already died by that time, but the thirty or so of us who showed up enjoyed catching up with each other.

Dimmitt High School class reunion, 2018. I'm standing in the middle row, second from the left.

My year in Texas passed quickly. I immensely enjoyed my time with all the members of the Bell family and we remain friends. In fact,

Kathy and I visited with Mike, Rick, and Lori's family[19] in September 2022 (Jeff was unable to join us since he lives in a different city).

After packing my things, the Bell family drove me to Brownwood, Texas, where we bid our farewells and I boarded a bus to tour a portion of the United States. I traveled through Texas, Arkansas, Missouri, Indiana, Ohio, Pennsylvania, New York, Massachusetts, Connecticut, New Jersey, and finally, Washington, D.C., where I caught a flight to São Paulo, Brazil.

I happily await my tour of a portion of the United States. Bus terminal, Brownwood, Texas, July 1968.

THE IMPORTANCE OF CONNECTIONS

Upon my return to Brazil, I had to complete my Brazilian high school requirements. Even though I had earned a high school diploma in the United States, my native country required me to complete one more semester of school before they would award me a Brazilian diploma.

---

19 Lori had passed away a few years prior to our trip.

In Brazil, the school year starts in March and runs through December, so when I came back from the U.S. in August, I still had four months remaining of my senior year. I completed the requirement at my old high school in Ribeirão Bonito.

Luzia, being older than me, had already graduated by the time I returned. She was the first woman and I was the first man in our family history to obtain high school diplomas, which opened doors to careers that we had never envisioned.

After graduating (again) in December 1968, I moved to São Paulo, where I enrolled in a preuniversity program (Curso Universitario) at Praça 14 Bis to study preengineering. The program was not a requirement to get into college, but it enhanced one's chances at the entrance examination. I shared an apartment with three other students from Ribeirão Bonito: Alvaro Ianhez, Afonso Celso Ianhez, and Josmar Verillo. We got along well and were thankful to be able to share living expenses, but we still had to work to meet our financial obligations, which also included our education.

A reunion with my former São Paulo roommates, circa 2000s.
L–R: Afonso Celso Ianhez, Josmar Verillo, Alvaro Ianhez, me, Estevan Ianhez.

A postcard depicting an aerial view of São Paulo, circa 1980s.

When I mentioned to my U.S. host father that I was looking for a job during one of our routine phone conversations, he referred me to the general manager of the Texaco company in São Paulo. Since Lonnie and this gentleman had once been members of the same church, he gave me the man's name and encouraged me to go talk with him. So I did.

He didn't have any part-time jobs, but he pointed to the building across the street and said, "That building contains the LICYLL, an English- and French-language institute for professionals preparing to go to other countries. I think that's a place you could use the English you just learned in the U.S. Why don't you go check it out?"

I went over and it was exactly as he said. I met a couple of people who had also participated in the AFS program in the U.S., and they hired me to teach English. The position offered me the flexibility to teach in the evenings so I could attend my classes and study during the day. I taught there for five years and became the director of programs.

Each of my classes were limited to ten people but included a diversity of professionals ranging from engineers and physicians to business executives and musicians. One of my students in 1969 stood out from the others. Dona Deoclecia do Prado Bento ("Dona Deo"), unlike most of the other students, had enrolled to learn English simply for her own personal education rather than a way to climb the corporate ladder. Soon she requested private classes, which I provided at a higher rate.

This was also the time period when I was completing my pre-college coursework (Curso Universitario) and realizing that engineering wasn't the right career path for me. I switched my focus to business and began applying to business schools. I was accepted to both Fundacão Getulio Vargas—EAESP (FGV—the top school) and PUC (a Catholic university that was less expensive). When Dona Deo asked me which school I was going to choose, I replied that I'd have to attend PUC for financial reasons.

"Don't do that," she admonished. "I want you to go to the top school. It's very important; you're a touchstone. You're going to go to FGV."

The next day, she called me to share that she and her husband, who operated a successful construction company and owned about twenty-five rental properties all over São Paulo, had agreed to give me the income from one of those properties every month to pay for my college tuition.

I was shocked and humbled. When I protested, she replied, "You need help, and we're happy to help. We want you to use it for your tuition."

Wow! Can you believe they paid for my tuition to the top school for the full two years? I'm still amazed by their generosity.

Kathy and I visited Dona Deo and her husband, Dr. Antonio Monteiro Machado, when we lived in São Paulo in the 1980s.

IMAGINATION AT ITS BEST

My willingness in the mid-1960s to take a chance on AFS by leaving all that was familiar and comfortable to me was a substantial risk—and it changed my life for the better. It allowed me, only eighteen at the time, to mature quickly and broaden my horizons. It gave me a tool (teaching English) to pay for college in Brazil, and it provided me the opportunity to start thinking beyond engineering. It also allowed me to meet Dona Deo, who was instrumental in getting me to the top business school. AFS was indeed "imagination at its best."

The Big Picture

1960s Overview

WORLD / U. S. [20]

- Dow:[21] 679.36–800.36, +18%
- Counterculture prevails; revolutions in social norms, clothing, music, drugs, sexuality, formalities, civil rights, schooling, social order, and relaxation of taboos (social mores)
- Advent of the "Red Army Faction" (Germany) and Zengakuren (Japan)
- U.S. has four Presidents: Eisenhower, Kennedy, Johnson, and Nixon
- U.S.S.R. has two leaders: Khrushchev and Brezhnev
- Johnson launches War on Poverty and Great Society programs
- Cuban Missile Crisis is averted in 1962
- Assassinations in the U.S.: JFK, Robert Kennedy, and MLK

BRAZIL

- Brasília is inaugurated in 1961
- Brazil wins soccer World Cup in Chile in 1962
- Brazil rotates through multiple presidents until the military takes over on March 31, 1964; stays until 1985
- The military regime seems to strike the right tone in the early years but becomes harsh late in the decade
- Brazilian economic miracle occurs between 1968–1974

---

[20] Source of historical data in this section: "1960s," Wikimedia Foundation, https://en.wikipedia.org/wiki/1960s. Last accessed September 25, 2023.

[21] Source of the Dow range in this section: "Dow Jones Industrial Average," Wikimedia Foundation, https://en.wikipedia.org/wiki/Dow_Jones_Industrial_Average. Last accessed October 24, 2023.

- Counterculture affects Brazil, too

PERSONAL SIGNIFICANT EVENTS / ACHIEVEMENTS

- Lives in Ribeirão Bonito, Brazil (2x); Dimmitt, Texas; São Paulo, Brazil
- Moves from the sitio to Ribeirão Bonito on January 20, 1959
- Becomes top student and learns English
- Becomes an AFS exchange student in Dimmitt, Texas, U.S.
- Moves to São Paulo to attend college
- Becomes an English teacher at LICYLL institute
- Is accepted to FGV/EAESP

3

TRIUMPH THROUGH SCHOLARSHIPS

The 1970s was the decade of higher education for me, starting in March 1970 at the Getulio Vargas Foundation. This Brazilian university and think tank, often abbreviated as FGV and also known as EAESP (São Paulo School of Business Administration), was established in 1954 with the mission to "stimulat[e] the country's economic development and social welfare."[22]

FGV required a lot of work and I dedicated myself fully to it. I made a concerted effort to be the top student all around and my hard work paid off in 1971 when I received the Premio Gastão Vidigal award. Named after a successful Brazilian banker and businessman, it was given to the top student from each of the University of São Paulo's four schools and FGV/EAESP.

---

[22] "Who We Are," the Brazilian Institute of Economics' website, https://portalibre.fgv.br/en/who-we-are. Last accessed November 7, 2023.

Announcement of winners of Premio Gastão Vidigal in the local newspaper, *Folha de São Paulo*, August 23, 1971.

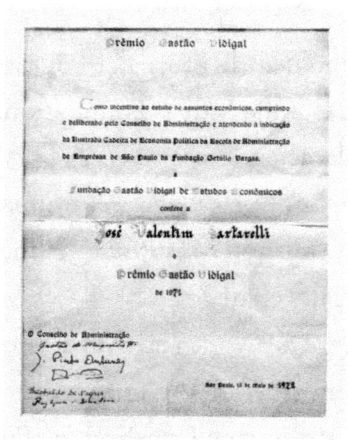

My Premio Gastão Vidigal award, 1971.

I believe that when you're good at what you do, you will get recognized. To be successful, you just have to commit yourself to the task at hand and be willing to put in the work.

And work I did. I attended my college classes from seven in the morning until one in the afternoon and taught English at the language institute from seven until eleven o'clock at night. During my final two years at FGV, my teaching expanded to include the Instituto Roosevelt and eventually the prebusiness program for students aiming to enter FGV.

In addition, I was required to complete an internship before graduation. During my senior year, one of my professors of economics, Dr. Luiz Carlos Bresser-Pereira,[23] invited me to intern under him at the Supermercados Pão de Açúcar, of which he was also the administrative director. It was the biggest supermarket chain in Brazil and where I learned a great deal about business and economics.

TRAGIC LOSS

On March 17, 1970, shortly after entering FGV, I lost my second-oldest sister Isaura, who died in a car accident that also killed her husband, Darcy Rocha, their nine-month-old daughter, Christiane, and a friend who was riding with them.

They were in a small Volkswagen Beetle on their way to Christiane's doctor appointment when a truck driver decided to pass them. Unfortunately, there was another truck coming from the opposite direction. Rather than swerving to the left, the truck driver threw his truck to the right, directly on top of my sister's car.

The loss was devastating to my family, particularly my mother and two sisters.

CONNECTIONS THROUGH TRANSLATION

Because of my job teaching English at the LICYLL, the administrators at FGV asked me to serve as an occasional translator for two

[23] Ten years later, he became Brazil's minister of finance.

Michigan State University professors, Dr. Donald A. Taylor and Dr. Leo G. Erickson, when they came to São Paulo to lecture at a major conference.

Dr. Taylor had frequently worked in Brazil since the 1950s in conjunction with FGV. His efforts were very much in line with what President Getúlio Vargas was trying to attain: a way to educate and train business professionals in order to establish and maintain a capitalist (free market) economy. In 1954, their efforts culminated in the creation of the Getulio Vargas Foundation—Escola de Administração de Empresas de São Paulo (FGV/EAESP). That creation was a "forceful means for the institution of teaching administration, of which Brazil lacks."[24]

As the chair of the Department of Marketing at the College of Business at Michigan State University, Dr. Taylor was selected to oversee the development of the new FGV business school in Brazil. He remained active in that position throughout the 1960s and 1970s, which is why he and Dr. Erickson, his colleague and friend, were still speaking in São Paulo while I was studying there.

I agreed to be their translator, which required me to stand on stage beside them and interpret what they said to an audience of corporate executives. It was mostly consecutive translation rather than simultaneous translation.

Serving as their translator was the beginning of a wonderful, long-standing academic relationship with them that would soon extend far beyond Brazil.

---

[24] Donald A. Taylor, *Institution Building in Business Administration—The Brazilian Experience* (MSU: International Business and Economic Studies, 1968), 3.

AN ECONOMIC SHIFT

Although I had initially supported the country's military government in the 1960s, I became disenchanted around 1972/1973 because they had become too harsh, imprisoning a lot of people simply for speaking out against their policies and actions. The reality was that if you said *anything* negative about the federal government, you would be identified and picked up for investigation ... and sometimes disappear forever. It made me a lifetime proponent of the right to free speech.

But not everything in Brazil was negative during this time. The national soccer team (Seleção Canarinha) won the World Cup in Mexico in 1970,[25] and the team's superstar, Pelé, continued to shine throughout the first half of the decade. In 1972, Brazil marked its sesquicentennial, which was celebrated in cities throughout the country. I shared an apartment with Josmar Verillo, one of my friends from Praça Mario Margarida, and our windows from the twenty-second floor offered a perfect view of the parades and festivities happening along the thoroughfare below, Avenida Paulista.

Most importantly, however, our country benefited from the economic impact of industrialization through such policies as import substitution, which served to launch car manufacturing in the late 1950s,[26] and major infrastructure projects such as Itaipu Dam during the Brazilian economic miracle of 1968–1974.

---

[25] The Seleção Canarinha has now won five times—1958, 1962, 1970, 1994, and 2002. This is more than any other country in the world.

[26] Rather than only importing cars from the U.S., Germany, and France, Brazil began to also make its own vehicles.

PLANNING FOR THE FUTURE

During my senior year at FGV, I began to think about enrolling in an MBA program because I believed that more education would take me further in my career. Knowing that I wanted to attend graduate school in the United States, several of my professors and the director of the university recommended that I apply for a Fulbright Scholarship to help me fund my dream.

The application process was similar to that of the AFS in which you submit a bunch of information, take a test, and then wait. The difference, however, was that the AFS selection was primarily based on the applicant's responses to one hundred questions while the Fulbright placed more weight on overall qualifications such as the classes taken, grades received, and what the applicant hoped to do with the MBA after graduation.

After earning my Bachelor of Business Administration degree from FGV in 1973, I learned I was in contention for a Fulbright Scholarship and began to apply to several universities. Once again, Dona Deo stepped in to help me financially, this time paying for the miscellaneous fees surrounding student visas and other government documentation.

My hope was to receive the scholarship, but as a backup plan, I set a goal of saving U.S.$10,000 by the time the final Fulbright determinations were made the following spring. I believed that amount would cover at least 60 percent of my MBA expenses if the scholarship did not work out.

Toward that effort, I accepted a paid internship position with AOLA, a consulting and market research company owned by its namesake, Dr. Alberto Oliveira Lima Filho, a highly regarded professor at FGV. My work at AOLA consisted of market planning and market research for political campaigns and a variety of commercial business ventures, including shopping centers in São Paulo, Osasco, and Rio. Shopping centers quickly rose in popularity in Brazil after the first one opened in 1964 and they continue to be popular today.

I learned that when building a shopping center, you first have to consider the anchor stores. Back then, common choices were Sears and Pernambucanas—large stores with wide appeal. Then you select the smaller stores in the middle of the shopping center, making sure there's a good mix of items being sold. Each company has to be identified, studied, and then pitched.

For example, I might contact Sears and say, "I'm developing a shopping center and I'm expecting to have a million people here. We'd love to have you become one of the anchor stores. This is the space we have, and this is the rent we're going to charge."

I enjoyed the internship, which lasted about a year. Then, in spring 1974, I received the wonderful news that I had been selected as a Fulbright scholar. Since Fulbright did not have its own money for all the scholarships it awarded, it sought outside funding from universities or foundations. In my case, General Electric Foundation gave them enough money to pay for my tuition and living expenses for all two years (in the end, I saved them money since I finished in just a year and a half).

This incredible gift enabled me to invest the $10,000 I had indeed managed to save. It was my first foray into investments, and I chose to place the money in CDs (certificate of deposits) for two years to take advantage of the 14 percent interest rate, which was quite high. I continued to invest in CDs throughout the 1970s and early 1980s.

Now that I had the scholarship, the next question was, Which school should I attend? I had been accepted by Indiana and a few other universities, but Michigan State University—my school of choice—had not yet responded. So I called Dr. Taylor, who was still the chair of the Department of Marketing at Michigan State's business school, and said, "I got the scholarship and I'd like to come, but I have not yet heard from MSU."

The next day, I learned that I was accepted.

All these experiences taught me that poverty is no reason for despair. If you are physically healthy, the fact that you're poor should not prevent you from obtaining an education and acquiring meaningful work. Being flexible, adaptable, and taking reasonable risks will help you achieve your goals.

MBA LIFE

With classes set to start in mid-September 1974, I left Brazil in late August so I could visit the Bell family in Dimmitt, Texas, before settling in at Michigan State University. During my week there, I also spoke to various civic organizations about the economic climate of Brazil.

By this time, I had grown long hair in keeping with the trending style. I didn't adopt any other hippie practices, but I did like having long hair. When disco hit in the latter half of the 1970s, it forced us to clean up our act.

I then made my way to East Lansing, Michigan, where I moved into Owen Hall, the coed dormitory reserved for the university's masters and PhD students.

TRIUMPH THROUGH SCHOLARSHIPS   49

'Zito' is back in town, is now Fulbright scholar

August 29, 1974 — CCN

"Zito" Sartarelli, who was an American Field Service exchange student at Dimmitt High School in 1967-68, is back in town this week.

THE YOUNG Brazilian is staying with the Lonnie Bells, his American AFS family, and is making the "luncheon circuit," telling local civic clubs about his country and the events of his life since his year in Dimmitt.

Sartarelli is about to start an exciting new chapter in his education. He has won a Fulbright Scholarship to Michigan State University's graduate business school. He will leave Dimmitt Sept. 9 and report to MSU at East Lansing on Sept. 16.

By attending classes winter and summer, he hopes to receive his master's degree in a year and a half, then push toward his PhD degree. His scholarship money is coming from the General Electric Foundation.

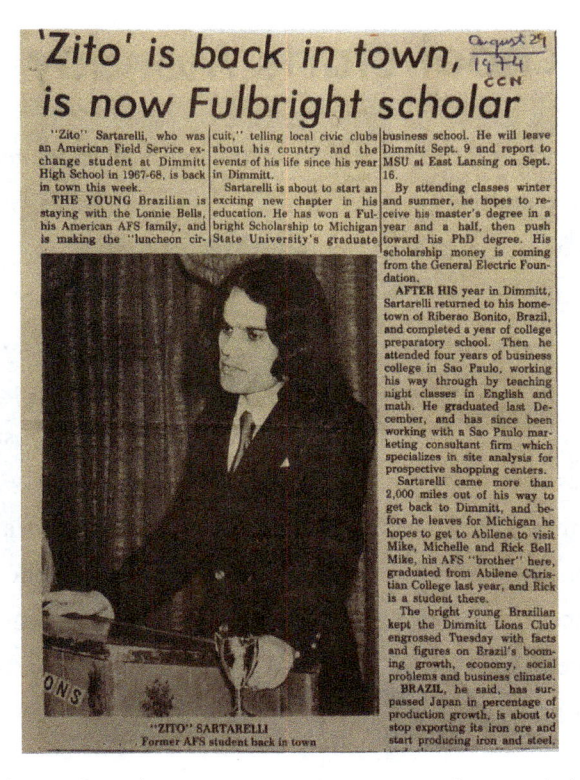

AFTER HIS year in Dimmitt, Sartarelli returned to his hometown of Riberao Bonito, Brazil, and completed a year of college preparatory school. Then he attended four years of business college in Sao Paulo, working his way through by teaching night classes in English and math. He graduated last December, and has since been working with a Sao Paulo marketing consultant firm which specializes in site analysis for prospective shopping centers.

Sartarelli came more than 2,000 miles out of his way to get back to Dimmitt, and before he leaves for Michigan he hopes to get to Abilene to visit Mike, Michelle and Rick Bell. Mike, his AFS "brother" here, graduated from Abilene Christian College last year, and Rick is a student there.

The bright young Brazilian kept the Dimmitt Lions Club engrossed Tuesday with facts and figures on Brazil's booming growth, economy, social problems and business climate.

BRAZIL, he said, has surpassed Japan in percentage of production growth, is about to stop exporting its iron ore and start producing iron and steel.

"ZITO" SARTARELLI
Former AFS student back in town

A clipping from the *Castro County News* announcing my scholarship status and return to Dimmitt, Texas, for a week to visit my AFS host family. August 29, 1974.

This photo of me was taken shortly after my arrival at Michigan State University; Owen Hall is in the background. Fall 1974.

Once the semester started, I was finally able to focus exclusively on my classes without having to work. My courses ranged from marketing and finance to operations research and management, and in all of them I studied hard, wrote great papers, and received excellent grades—some of the best of my MBA cohort.

My leadership skills kicked in, too. I established the Brazilian Student Association that organized parties and carnivals, which I was able to put together through fundraising efforts. Unfortunately, when the Brazilian Student Association held its first election, I lost the presidency. It was very disappointing.

Determined to finish my MBA a semester early, I applied for a PhD in business administration at MSU and began the search for funding since the Fulbright only covered my MBA expenses.

In December 1975, I obtained my master's degree a semester early as planned.

PHD LIFE AND A DELAYED CAREER

As soon as I began my PhD program, I approached Dr. Donald Bowersox, who was starting a sales forecasting project regarding supply chain issues. I knew that Dr. Bowersox had received grants from Whirlpool and other companies that allowed him to pay four PhD candidates to work as research associates and I asked to be one of them. He hired me as part of the team, along with David Closs, Tom Metzer, and Jeff Sims. We worked together for about a year until I decided to shift from supply chain to marketing and become a teaching assistant. I taught two classes (Marketing Introduction and Sales) as I continued my PhD program.

During this time, I also applied for and was awarded a CAPES Scholarship (Coordinação de Aperfeiçoamento do Pessoal de Nível Superior) from the Brazilian government. This matched my $1,500 per month teaching salary for three years, enabling me to quit teaching and focus only on my PhD, which I hoped to complete sometime in 1979.

In the midst of all of this, I allowed myself some downtime, too. Since I enjoyed playing soccer and there were several other Brazilian students living at Owen Hall, I initiated an intramural international soccer team consisting of Brazilians, Dutch, Americans, Kenyans, Brits, and others. It was a great way to get to know other students, exercise, and vent some stress.

The inaugural international soccer team of Owen Hall at MSU.
I'm the first person on the left, standing. Fall 1977.

By the end of 1977, I completed the coursework for the PhD and was preparing for the dissertation. I asked Dr. Taylor to become chair of my dissertation committee, which he graciously accepted. The dissertation focused on the growth of single-person households in America and the implications for companies and the business world. As an illustration, in 1960, only 13 percent of households were occupied by one person, typically those aged 65 or older.[27] That number has been growing significantly and accounts for over a quarter (27.6%) of all U.S. households in 2020.[28] Almost a third of all households are inhabited by single households, forcing consumer product companies to adapt to this new reality of the marketplace.

ANOTHER TRAGIC LOSS

I went home to Brazil every other year to visit family, and in December 1977, I was there for Christmas. Everyone was glad to see me, but my father was especially happy that I was back for a couple of weeks, that I was making great progress in my PhD, and that I had plans to return to Brazil after I finished my education.

On December 30, father was returning from the sitio in the late afternoon, riding in his little horse-drawn buggy along the side of the road. He was about one hundred yards from the entrance of the city when a car hit him from behind, killing him and the horse.

The driver was the daughter of one of our closest family friends. She claimed that the late-afternoon sun was shining in her eyes, preventing her from seeing him as she inadvertently drifted onto the shoulder of the road.

It was one of the worst days of my life. I had come to visit my father, a man whom I valued and loved, and I lost him. At least I was with my family and we were able to share our grief together, but his passing left a horrible void in my life.

---

27 José V. Sartarelli, "A Market Segmentation Study of Single (1-person) Householders by Demographic and Life Style Characteristics" (PhD dissertation, MSU, 1979), 45.

28 Lydia Anderson et al., "Home Alone: More Than a Quarter of All Households Have One Person," United States Census Bureau, June 8, 2023, https://www.census.gov/library/stories/2023/06/more-than-a-quarter-all-households-have-one-person.html.

My father was a man who valued tradition, honesty, and hard work. He believed that trust was one of the most honorable attributes a man or woman could possess. He was a loving father and generous to others, opening his arms to those who needed help, family or otherwise. Yet he wasn't a man who lived a life of ease. In addition to the manual labor required on the farm, the severed relationship with his brother, Tito, was very hard on him.

As for my mother, Alzira, the tragedies of first losing one of her daughters and then her husband affected her profoundly yet made her stronger and prepared her well for other things to come.

AN ACT OF CHIVALRY

One Sunday morning in 1978, I was sitting in the ground-floor atrium of Owen Hall reading the *New York Times* when I noticed a young woman enter and walk to the newspaper machine. I had seen her the day before, walking with who I presumed were her parents and sister. As she struggled to get a copy of the newspaper out of the machine, I approached to help. The machine was tricky; it would accept your coins, but unless you shook it, it would not allow access to the paper.

After I successfully retrieved a copy for her, I introduced myself and learned that she was Katherine Ann Strong, a new student coming in from Penn State to get a master's degree and PhD in biophysics. I offered to show her around the campus, which she accepted, and that was the beginning of a love story that continues today.

After we had been dating for a while, I was introduced to her parents, Richard and Rowena Strong. Richard was an internationalist who had received his undergraduate degree at the University of

Michigan and had been working toward a PhD in geology until he was hired by U.S. Steel as a geologist in 1946. Back then, U.S. Steel was one of the biggest companies in the world, with their headquarters in Pittsburgh, Pennsylvania. He stayed with that company until he retired in 1982.

His work took him to Spain, Mexico, Peru, and Iran but most extensively to Brazil because it is home to the largest iron ore deposit in the world—the Serra Norte Mining Complex in the Carajás Mountains. Richard Strong was the second person to step foot on that deposit site when it was discovered in the mid-1960s.[29]

Richard loved Brazil, he said, because the people were so nice to him. That was particularly true of a hotel in Rio de Janeiro called Ouro Verde, whose hospitality kept him coming back as a loyal customer for years on end. I was glad he was able to see Rio when it was such a lovely city and offered all kinds of good things, including fewer people and *favelas* (slums or shantytowns).

Rowena and their three girls weren't able to travel with Richard on his international assignments since he was sent to undeveloped land and major construction sites for three months at a time. The Serra Norte Mining Complex, for example, is in the middle of nowhere in the Amazon jungle. He always brought souvenirs back for each of his ladies, though.

Since Richard was very interested and involved in economic development, we had many wonderful conversations over the years and shared a mutual respect for each other.

---

29 U.S. Steel owned 50 percent of the site; the other half was owned by the Brazilian company, Vale. In the central part of the complex, they built a railroad that extends nine hundred kilometers to the port. It's just an amazing development. Eventually, U.S. Steel sold all their holdings to Vale in an effort to save themselves.

ACADEMIA VS. CORPORATE AMERICA

As I finished my dissertation, I considered my future. I debated whether I should go into academia, which was the natural profession for someone with a PhD, or go into business, a path out of the ordinary. I interviewed with many universities and got an offer to be an assistant professor at Auburn University, but after five-and-a-half years at Michigan State, I was tired of the academic environment. I really did not want to teach the same syllabus for thirty-five years and then retire, only to wish that I had done something else.

I leaned more toward the corporate environment, which seemed to offer a vast diversity of opportunities, people, and locations. I sent out 141 resumes, received about 35 responses, and interviewed with several companies including Eli Lilly, Merck, Pfizer, Dow Chemical, Duracell, and Corning Glass. Two good offers came back: one from Eli Lilly and another from Merck.

Merck, at that time in 1979, was the number one pharmaceutical company in the U.S. and Lilly was in the top ten. The deciding factor came down to location and mutual ties.

Merck was based in Rahway, New Jersey, and Eli Lilly was in Indianapolis. After visiting both, I liked Indianapolis better. In addition, during the application process with Lilly, I interviewed with Don Joyce, vice president of their Latin American operations. He had graduated from Michigan State and was very interested in getting another Spartan to join his company. Even more importantly, Lilly met the three expectations I had for my future employer: it was strong in marketing, it sold products internationally, and it had a strong presence in Brazil specifically.

It was my desire to return to Brazil to work in order to "repay" the Brazilian government for my CAPES scholarship. It wasn't anything they required; I simply wanted to do it to honor the confidence they had in me. So I looked for companies that were very profitable and that had operations in Brazil. If they had a brand presence in Brazil with a sales office or a manufacturing plant, that was ideal. All the companies I interviewed with had maintained a successful presence in Brazil for many years, but Lilly stood above the rest to me.

I received Lilly's offer in mid-1979, and I agreed to accept it based on one condition: that I not start until January 1980. Don called me and said, "Zito, stop being a professional student and come join us in Indianapolis. I have a job waiting for you; I think you're going to do well here." As tempting as the offer was, I was more committed to finish my dissertation. I replied, "Don, thank you for your great interest in me. I apologize for not being able to join you now, but I have already invested three-and-a-half years of my life in earning a PhD, so I am going to finish what I started. Rest assured that in January 1980, I shall be there if the offer still stands."

My formal class photo at Michigan State University, fall 1979.

That fall, I successfully defended my dissertation and started planning for my future. I knew that I wanted Kathy to be a part of it, so I met with her father and asked for his blessing to marry her. Richard was happy to grant it and shortly thereafter, I proposed to Kathy at our dorm, Owen Hall.

In December 1979, I completed my PhD program as a newly engaged man and looked forward to the next chapter of my life.

At age thirty, I'm ready to attend my PhD graduation ceremony at Michigan State University on a cold winter day. December 12, 1979.

IMAGINATION AT ITS BEST

I am proof that "it takes a village" to grow talent. Starting with the AFS Scholarship in 1967/1968, followed by the help provided by Dona Deo and Dr. Antonio so I could attend FGV, the Fulbright Scholarship funded by the General Electric Foundation so I could earn my MBA, the research/teaching assistantships at Michigan State University, and the CAPES Scholarship which allowed me to finish my PhD, scholarships and other financial help have been foundational for my success.

The question one may ask is, Why would a young boy, born and raised on a farm in the interior of Brazil, seek scholarships and private donors to help him with his education? A linear reading of my background would indicate that I would not be interested in such assistance. Indeed, most of my siblings were not interested in education. However, a nonlinear approach to life allowed me to accomplish things educationally that very few people have done. Two things were critical to my achievements: there was a will to be educated, and there was a commitment to work hard to change the trajectory of my life.

The Big Picture

1970s Overview

WORLD / U. S. [30]

- Dow:[31] 800.36–838.74, +4.8%
- World confronted by oil crisis
- Pinochet takes over in Chile in 1973
- Stagflation becomes a reality
- Quantum field theory
- "Me" decade with excessive individualism vs. communitarianism
- Death of Mao Tse-tung in 1976 and emergence of Deng Xiaoping who would bring some market economics to China
- Nixon resignation; surfacing of Ford; appearance of Jimmy Carter
- Japan now second-largest economy, surpassing Germany
- Iranian Revolution; U.S. hostages in Iran
- Green revolution advances economies; oil crisis holds them back
- Frequent coups, wars, domestic conflicts, and civil wars brought about by disputes between the West and U.S.S.R.
- Progressivism continues to spread
- Thatcher becomes Prime Minister in 1979

BRAZIL

- Médici, Geisel, and João Figueiredo take turns as Presidents of Brazil

---

30 Source of historical data in this section: "1970s," Wikimedia Foundation, https://en.wikipedia.org/wiki/1970s. Last accessed September 25, 2023.

31 Source of the Dow range in this section: "Dow Jones Industrial Average," Wikimedia Foundation, https://en.wikipedia.org/wiki/Dow_Jones_Industrial_Average. Last accessed October 24, 2023.

- Brazilian economic miracle (1968–1974) underway; GDP growth close to 10% per year
- Great celebrations of Brazil's sesquicentennial in 1972
- Brazil wins soccer World Cup in Mexico in 1970; Pelé plays for U.S. Cosmos in 1974
- Import substitution is one of government's initiatives to expand growth; the other, borrowing

PERSONAL SIGNIFICANT EVENTS / ACHIEVEMENTS

- Lives in São Paulo, Brazil; East Lansing, Michigan
- Fundacão Getulio Vargas (FGV/EAESP), top student
- English Teacher (5 years), LICYLL, Instituto Roosevelt, CPV (Curso de Preparação Vestibular, FGV)
- Premio Gastão Vidigal, political economy, 1971 (one of top five students of economics in São Paulo, FGV/EAESP and the University of São Paulo)
- Interns at Supermercados Pão de Açúcar for Bresser Pereira (future Minister of Finance)
- Interns for pay at AOLA (Antonio de Oliveira Lima Filho)
- Translates for Dr. Donald Taylor and Dr. Leo Erickson
- Becomes a Fulbright scholar and completes an MBA at Michigan State University
- Meets Katherine Ann Strong, future wife, in 1978
- Obtains a PhD in business administration
- Decides to pursue a corporate career instead of an academic one

LOSSES

- Sister Isaura and her family, March 17, 1970
- Father Joáo Sartarelli, December 30, 1977

4

FIGHTING THE GOOD FIGHT

The year 1980 was particularly pivotal for me, full of changes and new opportunities. It was the year I got my first professional job, replaced my first car (a 1969 Impala) with an almost-new Buick Cutlass Supreme, moved to a new location, and, by year's end, had become a newly married man.

On January 7, 1980, at the age of thirty-one, I joined Eli Lilly and Company. As the decade progressed, I worked my way up in management through six consecutive positions within the company. Some patterns and progressions among those positions emerged:

- There were a few jobs where I was just learning the business—getting to know the products, the customers, and the interface between the two.
- Half were sales jobs in which I worked under the operational team; the other half made me a member of the operational team, overseeing sales as well as profitability.

- Two of my jobs included the management of multiple arms of the company, including pharmaceuticals, agricultural chemicals, and animal health products.
- Some of the positions were heavily involved in shaping the external environment on matters of intellectual property rights, pricing, and regulatory affairs.
- Finally, all the jobs were either in North America or Latin America but involved countries other than the one in which I was based.

Each of the positions challenged me and forced me to think and respond quickly. Throughout it all, I consistently looked for ways to improve the company's climate, cash flow, and productivity.

ELI LILLY AND COMPANY

Immediately after being hired, Lilly placed me in sales school for a month with five other men. All of them were pharmacists, which was customary back in those days for pharmaceutical sales positions; I was the only one with a PhD in business administration.

The six of us worked well together and played off each other's strengths. They knew more about anatomy, chemistry, and drug products than I did, but I knew more about business, accounting, marketing, and HR.

Dista Sales School graduates, Eli Lilly and Company, Indianapolis, IN, January 1980. Standing (L–R): Glenn Pangrazzi, Kent Palmore, Dave Wilson. Seated (L–R): Dave Grabenauer, me, Brian Carroll.

After completing sales school, we were required to work as sales reps for six months. The position offered base pay plus commission, as well as a company car—a beautiful new white Chevy Monte Carlo. I requested a territory in the warmer climes of California, Texas, or Florida and was given a 200-mile-long territory in western Texas that ran from Lubbock to Pecos.

My job was to clean up a small, metal box containing 300 index cards (my sales "list") by visiting the physicians on each card to learn more about them and determine whether they were viable clients. The caveat was that I had to maintain at least 250 names on the list; if I removed more than fifty, I had to find replacements.

Another challenge was scheduling. Often, the physicians were not there when I stopped by because they were on vacation or sick leave or traveling. If I was unable to meet with two of the twelve I had selected for the day, I had to rush to visit a few additional doctors before closing hours.

All the meetings needed to be effective as well, meaning I had to either ensure that the physicians would continue to prescribe Lilly's products or convince them to start prescribing them. This was difficult because every doctor already had two or three products they liked to prescribe for particular ailments and diseases. They didn't—and still don't—consider ten products; they look at two or three, max. My job was to make sure Lilly's products occupied one of those coveted top-of-mind choices.

Due to the size of my territory, the sales position required extensive travel, but it was a great opportunity to see the business up close. I learned a great deal and quickly became an effective sales rep. However, sales is one of the toughest jobs in the world. Either you become good at it or you give up.

Since Lubbock was only seventy miles from Dimmitt, Texas, where I had lived for a year during high school, I was able to visit the Bell family occasionally on weekends.

By the end of June, I concluded my prerequisite sales assignment and was sent back to Indianapolis to intern in both sales training and marketing research, which I enjoyed very much.

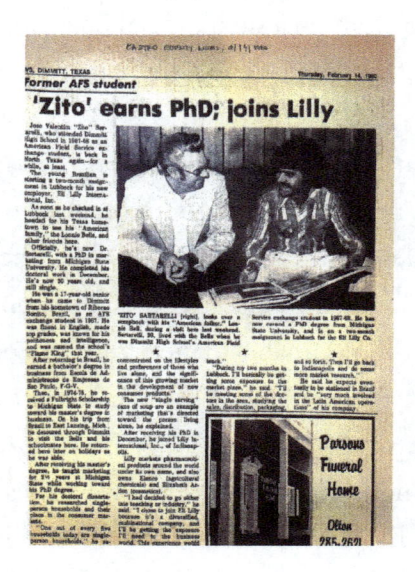

Lonnie Bell and I chat during my visit. "'Zito' earns PhD; joins Lilly," *Castro County News*, February 14, 1980.

WEDDING BELLS

I graduated in December 1979 and moved to Indianapolis after Christmas. Kathy remained in East Lansing, Michigan, for about eight months to finish up her master's degree. During Kathy's April visit to Lubbock while I was on my sales assignment, we discussed plans for the wedding and set the date for September 6, 1980, at her family's Episcopal Church in Pittsburgh, Pennsylvania.

Since I am Catholic and Kathy is Episcopalian, I had to get a dispensation from the Catholic Church to allow me to get married in her church. Kathy's mother was very helpful in obtaining the dispensation, which took a lot of meetings and persuasion. At the ceremony, a Catholic priest and an Episcopal minister officiated together.

Sartarelli wedding. L–R: Sarah Strong (Kathy's younger sister), Susan Strong (Kathy's older sister), Kathy, me, Dr. Donald Taylor, and Bruce Arnt (one of my friends from university). Episcopal Church, Pittsburgh, PA, September 6, 1980.

Kathy's oldest sister Susan served as her maid of honor and Dr. Taylor served as my best man. None of my family members were able to travel from Brazil to attend, but we sent them wedding invitations printed in Portuguese and lots of pictures.

We enjoyed a big reception, followed by a honeymoon to Paris and Rome. During the overnight train ride between the two cities, we shared a sleeping compartment with four other people—two nuns and another couple. The nuns positioned themselves in the top bunks, which didn't pose a problem until they took their shoes off. The unpleasant odor was inescapable.

The honeymoon was a great trip that began a shared lifelong love of travel. We flew back to Pittsburgh to pick up our car and drove to Indianapolis. I had turned thirty-one by this point and was determined to work hard at my job and successfully share my life with Kathy.

INDIANAPOLIS

Indianapolis has always been a beautiful city, but back then, we didn't bother venturing out after eight o'clock at night since its downtown didn't have much—I remember one Hilton Hotel and the Athletic Club and that was about it. Now it's one of the best cities in America with all kinds of restaurants, museums, performing-arts centers, and so forth.

Kathy and I moved into an apartment on the north side of Indianapolis where we made friends and frequently played racquetball and tennis. We also began preparing for an international move since I had been told that my current position at headquarters would last no more than a year and a half.

Since Lilly's headquarters is located downtown, I liked to leave early for work, around six thirty, which typically allowed me to get to the office by seven o'clock. If I waited to leave at eight, it would take me an hour to get there due to rush hour. Often, I carpooled with four or five other new hires.

The first few months were unpredictable but exciting. The team I was on helped prepare the launch of new products in various countries and reviewed the results of market research in order to make recommendations to management. Working for a variety of international executives with different management styles caused concerns for some of us coming from university backgrounds who were accustomed to working under only one person.

Kathy and I spent Christmas that year (1980) in Pittsburgh and from that time on, we alternated the holidays each year between the U.S. and Brazil. Fortunately, my family didn't have to wait until the following Christmas to finally meet Kathy. In spring 1981, we flew to Brazil for a brief visit before settling into Caracas, Venezuela, where I had accepted a new position as manager of marketing development for Lilly Pharma.

Sartarelli family at home in Ribeirão Bonito, S.P., Brazil, in the early 1980s. L–R: Carlito, Tilim, Cidinha, Alzira, Luzia, me.

Sartarelli family ladder of cousins at Ribeirão Bonito, S.P., Brazil, in the early 1980s. L–R: Me, Conceicão, Juninho, Evandro, Marcio, Joseane, Ana Paula, Cesar.

LILLY VENEZUELA

Prior to leaving the States, Kathy and I were sent to the inlingua school in Cincinnati, Ohio, to learn Spanish. She had taken four years of the language in high school and I spoke Portuguese, so within two weeks, we became fairly proficient in the language.

I also requested American expat status from Eli Lilly so that I would be paid in U.S. dollars rather than Venezuelan bolivares. Given the political and economic instabilities so prevalent in that part of the world, I wanted to ensure that our personal finances wouldn't be affected by any potential currency devaluations. Fortunately, even though I was not yet an American citizen, the company granted my request.[32]

---

[32] Most U.S. companies don't pay expatriates in American dollars anymore; you're much more likely to be paid in the local currency today.

When we lived in Venezuela, it was one of the best places to live and work in all Latin America. As home to one of the largest oil deposits in the world, it was a very rich country. It was also modern, ran smoothly under a democratic government, and enjoyed rapid economic development.

If you go to Venezuela today, however, you see only poverty. There is no resemblance now to the pleasant and welcoming country where Kathy and I spent thirteen months. Anyone who likes socialism should go there to see how poor governance has devastated it in such a short amount of time.

Time to Launch

Upon arrival in Caracas, I met my boss, Manolo Ripoll, an experienced manager with a high level of energy who provided me with tremendous support. Our Venezuelan operation was one of Lilly's smallest, selling just a few million dollars in products, but it was also used as a training ground for a lot of the company's executives, including me.

My job as the marketing-development manager was to oversee market planning and product launches, specifically for the new drug Ceclor®, which eventually became one of Lilly's top anti-infective products. My responsibilities included training a small sales force and supplying them with promotional materials and ongoing support.

It was a lot of work and involved many sales meetings, but I enjoyed my managerial role and anticipated the upward mobility Lilly offered.

The Car Accident

My office was in the capital city of Caracas, but I often traveled to our small factory in Maracay, just outside the capital. During one of those trips, I was joined by Manolo and another manager from our Caracas office. On our return trip that evening, Manolo was driving the Ford Marquis, the manager was sitting in the front passenger seat, and I was sitting in the back when Manolo had to suddenly swerve to avoid an oncoming car in our lane.

In the process, the oncoming car hit the center median, jumped over it, landed against a light pole, and hit us head on. Manolo, who was wearing his seatbelt, was fine. The manager was pushed partly underneath the glove compartment by the force of the impact, but, thankfully, wasn't severely injured. And I, who was not wearing my seatbelt, broke my left arm but thankfully remained in the backseat.

By the time we were released from the hospital, Lilly had arranged for a different car to be delivered to us and we made it back to Caracas by one o'clock in the morning. I arrived home with blood all over my shirt and my arm in a cast, but it could have been much worse.

Kathy and me at our home a few days after the car accident. Caracas, Venezuela, fall 1981.

Moving On

Kathy and I lived in a company-sponsored apartment with a nice view in the small neighborhood of Santa Rosa de Lima. Various shops, a *padaria* (bakery), and a grocery store were all within walking distance. We made lots of friends, both within the company and in the neighborhood. Dr. Robert Arrom, a longtime Venezuelan Lilly employee, was particularly welcoming to us and frequently hosted parties at his home, including an American-style Thanksgiving.

Venezuela offers a wonderful climate year-round, so Kathy and I frequently explored some of the country's beaches along the east coast and took day trips into the interior, visiting the sites associated with Simón Bolívar and the verdant Parque del Este botanic garden. We even took a cruise around the Caribbean.

Then, in June 1982, the company offered me the opportunity to become a general manager in Santiago, Chile.

I accepted.

LILLY / ELANCO CHILE

Chile at that time was under military rule, led by General Augusto Pinochet. Although it was a poor country, its economic posture was favorable to business, particularly since the country's leadership included a few economists who had trained at the University of Chicago.

Kathy and I moved into a wonderful apartment situated along a tree-lined street in the suburb of Providencia. We made many more friends and continued playing tennis; some of the courts offered fabulous views of the snow-covered Andes Mountains. We also attended company events, many of which were held in beautiful vineyards, and twice we enjoyed the Viña del Mar International Song Festival.

An Unenviable Task

My position as general manager placed me in direct report to Robert Barkei, who oversaw Lilly operations in several small Latin American countries and who, in turn, reported to Roy Cage, vice president for Latin America. I learned about business big time under their leadership. Roy, an experienced executive, was demanding but fair and helped me to think through various issues. He loved brainstorming with his team and he himself had great ideas that he was not shy to share. He believed in incentives and motivation and was interested in shaping the external environment. My later work in the 1990s on intellectual property rights, pricing, and regulatory affairs had his complete support.

Once again I was in charge of overseeing the launch of new products in a small market, but this time, I was assigned the additional task of making the organization profitable.

Since the company had sold many different agricultural chemicals, animal health products, and pharmaceutical products over the years, one of the first things I asked to see was the chart of accounts. I was dismayed to discover that not only was it unorganized but it was also incomplete. We had to rebuild the whole thing, which was a pain in the neck. Then we had to figure out how much money each account owed and create a process for collecting that money. That's right; no one had been collecting money, either.

To make things worse, as soon as Kathy and I arrived in Chile, the country was crushed by a 30–40 percent devaluation of the peso, which exposed the company's many uncollected receivables. In other words, when we imported products from the U.S. at $100, we owed them $100. But now all we could collect from our local customers was the equivalent of $60.

We immediately started collecting whatever money the customers could afford. This was made even more difficult since our competitors retained their existing pay-when-you-can policy. Since I wasn't permitted to talk to the competition regarding the matter, I sat down and began negotiating with the clients, preparing customized plans to collect their monies. It wasn't easy.

I also began to train the sales reps on how to collect money. "It's not a sale until it's collected," I said. "A sale that's not collected is actually a gift. Therefore, you have to help collect each sale." There was a lot of resistance initially, but over time, we successfully trained them to become efficient at both selling and collecting.

We also restructured the entire operation, capitalized on existing and new talented personnel, launched new products in all three lines, and constantly looked for more opportunities to grow the business.

The End of a Market

Despite our great gains and forward momentum, the $500 million market simply wasn't large enough for Lilly to retain. The company decided to exit Chile and promote me to the much larger Brazilian market.

Thus, two years after my arrival, my final assignment in Santiago was to secure licensing agreements for our products in order to exit the market. Following the successful transfer of our pharmaceutical product licenses to Pfizer and our animal health products and agricultural chemical licenses to Roche, Kathy and I departed for São Paulo, Brazil.

LILLY / DOW-ELANCO BRAZIL

In June 1984, I reported as director of pharmaceutical marketing planning and research to my boss, Edgar Schwantes, a highly experienced marketing professional. The expectation was that I would replace him as director of pharmaceutical operations when he retired, but first, my responsibilities included launching new products, conducting research, preparing marketing materials, and managing a small twenty-five-person team of product managers and market researchers.

The general manager of Lilly Brazil at that time was George Baumer. At one of my first sales meetings there, I watched as he carried a wooden crutch to the front of the room and broke it in front of everyone to emphasize that we should not rely on "crutches" when selling our products. It wasn't the best first impression he could have made on me, but it definitely set the tone and expectation for the future.

Executive meeting in Brazil, late 1980s. L–R: Robert Postlethwait, General Manager of Lilly-Elanco Brazil; Roy Cage, Vice President of Latin America, Asia Pacific, Commonwealth Countries; William Stanford, CFO of Roy Cage's area; and me as Director, Pharmaceutical Operations of Lilly Brazil.

Heralding the Truth

Edgar delegated well and allowed me to exercise my expertise, but in order to help grow sales and restore profitability to the pharmaceutical business, I first had to spend a lot of time convincing him that we were actually in the red financially and had been for several years.

The fact was that Lilly Brazil was selling well but losing money on every sale. Lilly headquarters informed me that unless this problem was rectified, they were going to close the Brazilian operations just as they had done in Chile. Now remember, this is my home country. I was determined to fix the problem. Plus, it's in my DNA. If I see something wrong, I like the challenge of fixing it.

Despite our low ranking of #22 in the market, Edgar and the other managers in Brazil thought our financial plight was fake news. "We're not losing money. We're making medicine!"

I did my best to convince them otherwise. "Look," I said. "I've reviewed the numbers both here and in Indianapolis. We are losing money at this very moment. We have to get our act together and turn the company around."

To their credit, even though they didn't believe me, they worked with me to do just that. Most of my time was spent in meetings, meetings, and more meetings—one after the other. We worked hard to resolve issues, cut through governmental red tape, simplify processes, grow sales, lower expenses, and collect as much money as possible. In short, we did more with less.

Inflation at that point was out of control; it had risen to 200 percent per year in 1982 and rose even more after Kathy and I arrived in 1984. Amid such hyperinflation, it was critical to get good prices for our products or else experience an even bigger cash-flow crisis.

Therefore, I focused on obtaining government approval to raise our prices. The sales price for each drug—and each dosage size—was tightly controlled by the government. It was a lot of paperwork, but we did it.

Advancement Opportunity

By the middle of 1986, Edgar Schwantes retired and I became director of pharmaceutical operations, which included marketing planning and research, sales training, and sales. I was now overseeing up to 400 sales reps, district sales managers, product managers, and market researchers.

I also remained responsible for growing sales and market share, improving prices vis-à-vis hyperinflation, focusing on motivation, and working on making the operations even more equitable than ever.

I recalled that back when I worked as a sales rep in Lubbock, Texas, Lilly had hired a woman as a sales rep for the Dallas region and she did a terrific job. So, I hired the first woman in the sales force for the district of São Paulo, which was revolutionary and the beginning of a trend. People started to understand that Lilly really meant business when we talked about gender equality.

However, it didn't come without its own set of challenges. For example, many sales meetings were held out of town, which meant the sales team stayed at hotels. Despite all members of the team being instructed not to do anything inappropriate, an incident occurred and we had to let go of our first female employee.

However, the subsequent women (and men) we hired made us proud. We acquired some excellent, talented individuals, and their contributions to the company were beneficial for all of us. Maybe other companies had more women than we did at that point, but the quality of our female reps was exceptional.

I continue to think hiring women is the right thing to do. It's imagination at its best, especially in a culture like Latin America, which did not initially see the value of women in sales positions. Office workers? Fine. But not salespeople. My hiring of those first few women was innovative and out of the box. It was an illustration of "fighting the good fight."

The Power of Motivation

Having been a salesman myself for a brief period of time, I knew motivation was critical for not only retaining our sales team, but also helping them meet their sales goals. I decided that an incentive program was in order and worked with several members of the management team to develop a performance-based incentive program focused on travel.

Some of our Brazilian-born sales reps had been working with us for twenty, thirty, or forty years and had never been out of the country. The opportunity to visit company headquarters in Indianapolis and attend an Indy 500 race or attend the 1986 soccer World Cup in Mexico was an experience not to be missed.

We made it abundantly clear to our sales reps that they were never allowed to incentivize the physicians into prescribing our products in order to reach their sales goals. This applied to all Lilly's markets worldwide. Anytime management learned that a salesperson had offered or provided any form of incentive to a client, that person immediately lost their job.

Thankfully, that rarely happened, and the salespeople worked "hard and right." All of it was truly exciting.

The Lost Decade

A foreign company can't operate inside a bubble within its host nation. Indeed, the politics and economics of Brazil impacted our Lilly operation in significant ways. As one of the company's top managers, I was on the front lines daily, working to creatively and flexibly overcome the severe challenges brought about by the Brazilian government and some of its policies.

After twenty-one years of military rule, the "Diretas Já" ("direct voting immediately") grassroots movement took hold in the mid-1980s. The people, the political parties, and the newspapers protested for a proper election without any military intervention or interference. Military leader and President João Figueiredo agreed to a democratic election and ultimately conceded defeat, turning the government over to Tancredo Neves in 1985. Unfortunately, Neves died before he could take office, causing José Sarney, who had been voted in as vice president, to assume the presidency.

The change in leadership also happened to coincide with an economic downturn. When the military had taken over in 1964, they adopted an open economy that allowed for capitalism to flourish, which enabled Brazil to develop very fast. Its gross domestic product grew at 9–10 percent a year—"the Brazilian economic miracle." That was positive, but they didn't have the funds to pay for all of it.

This caused the government to relax their regulations, which enticed international companies to come to Brazil and open offices—using their own money. That was positive, too. But the government didn't stop borrowing large amounts of money from banks and other institutions to build highways, infrastructure, and hydroelectric plants, which are still operational in Brazil today.

The loans weren't a problem until the economic downturn of the 1980s. Growth slowed and all of a sudden, the government owed a huge amount of money to foreign banks. In fact, multinational banks were said to be earning more than a quarter of their profits from Brazil alone during that time. So while the government had successfully created a solid infrastructure, it left Brazil with such massive debt that the 1980s became known as the "lost decade" because we were unable to invest and grow during that time.

To assist Brazil and so many other Latin American countries who found themselves in similar situations, the U.S. secretary of the treasury, Nicholas Brady, developed a new debt-reduction strategy called Brady bonds. In essence, Brady bonds were sovereign debt securities, denominated in U.S. dollars, issued by developing countries, and backed by U.S. Treasury bonds. They restored trust between the developing countries and the international financial community.

Because Brazil had so much external debt, a vast array of bonds was initiated, which introduced yet another problem: Brazil now had to resolve their massive debt issue in U.S. dollars, not its native currency of cruzeiros.[33] And that complicated situation extended to my work at Lilly.

For example, Lilly headquarters in the U.S. sold products to us in dollars. But I had to sell the products to the Brazilian people in cruzeiros. When the two currencies are solvent and balanced, it's not a problem. But at one point during that time, Brazil was suffering inflation of 50 percent *per month*, which led to frequent devaluations of the local currency. That was a huge problem because after I sold the products and collected in cruzeiros, I then had to go to the bank

---

33 Cruzeiro was the basic monetary unit of Brazil until 1986. Brazil launched the cruzado in 1986, followed by the cruzeiro real in 1993. The real became effective in 1994.

to exchange the cruzeiros into dollars so I could pay Lilly in the U.S. But since the cruzeiro was worth much less than the dollar, that meant I was always coming up short of what we owed Indianapolis.

In addition, it caused a crisis on payday. Originally we had paid employees monthly, but now we had to pay our employees two or three times a month. If we waited to pay them at the end of the month, their money would be worth 50 percent of what it used to be.

Inflation affects everybody, but it affects the poor the most. The country went into a morass as crime and poverty levels rose. Companies watched their purchasing power decline and couldn't adjust their employees' salaries fast enough. We tried to increase our employees' salaries every couple of months … until the minister of finance put an end to price and wage increases.

It was all very stressful, particularly for a manager.

In 1986, two years after my arrival and a year after the presidency transitioned from military to civilian, a new minister of finance was appointed. He happened to be someone I knew very well—Dr. Bresser Pereira, my professor at Getulio Vargas Foundation (FGV) and administrative director at Supermercados Pão de Açúcar. Unfortunately, Bresser's solution to stabilize the economy was to freeze bank accounts for six months with the promise of full repayment with interest. The only reason anyone was allowed to access their money was if they had a medical emergency.

At the time, Lilly was selling millions of dollars of products, but all that money was suddenly inaccessible for six months, regardless of the fact that I had about one thousand employees whose salaries I needed to pay. How was I going to do that? I looked at the cash we had on hand and immediately paid out what we could. We also tried to collect as much cash from customers as possible, but some of our customers didn't want to pay because they needed that money; the freeze was happening to them, too. It was all very troublesome, but we survived.

By the late 1980s, Brazil finally began to accumulate the necessary U.S. dollars by exporting twice as much as we imported. Eventually, all that debt was renegotiated and eliminated, but there was no money left over to invest.

The First Brazilian-Born General Manager

In 1988, I was promoted to general manager of Lilly/Elanco Brazil, the first Brazilian-born general manager in the history of the company. I continued to emphasize sales growth and the launch of new products for all lines of our company (pharmaceuticals, agricultural chemicals, and animal health), but my primary focus was on improving prices, intellectual property rights, and regulatory affairs.

Standing at my desk while serving as the new General Manager at Lilly/Dow-Elanco Brazil in 1988.

By this time, Lilly was granted some of the best price increases of anybody in the industry because we had learned how to justify our requests and effectively negotiate with the appropriate government officials. Nevertheless, the government always came up with modifications or changes to their regulations on Fridays. Every Friday, you could expect that something unusual would be announced. It was as if the government wanted to terrorize the businesspeople.

I traveled to Brasília frequently to convince the minister of health and the minister of commerce to double the price of one of our life-saving antibiotics, which then became a multimillion-dollar product because we sold so much of it. In addition, I capitalized on the fact that Keflex® was a quality product we manufactured locally (after importing the raw materials), a distinguishing feature from the competitors that enabled it to sell well.

I was also in charge of the launch of Prozac® 20 in Brazil. Prozac® became the blockbuster drug for Lilly worldwide, culminating in almost $4 billion in sales globally. The "20" was included in the product's name to remind physicians that 20 milligrams did the job. This was important because some of our other products had multiple sizes—it could be 5, 10, 20, 30, or 40 milligrams—which could lead to confusion. We decided to label it what doctors should be focusing on, which is 20 milligrams.

Prozac® launch team, Lilly Brazil, 1986. I am standing in the back row, second from right.

Lilly had started as a diabetic insulin company, later grew into a powerful antibiotic company as well, and then Prozac® placed us prominently in the central-nervous-system area of mental health.

The Power of Proper Training

New products were always launched in January, which required me to have an initial meeting with the director of marketing operations, sales managers, and product managers at the beginning of each year.

These regional managers would then go back to their respective territories to train their district managers, who in turn set up week-long meetings with their sales reps. I sent my product managers to each of those meetings to help educate the sales force about the new products and review the marketing plans. At the end of the training, the sales reps were ready to go, armed with samples, marketing materials, and new strategies.

To reinforce these initial trainings, we held quarterly meetings with the entire Lilly Brazil sales team and their managers at various locations throughout the country. These meetings were critical training events, but I incorporated fun into them as well, such as soccer games between sales teams in the late afternoons.

Our sales-incentive program continued but at this point, I also extended it to my direct reports; directors and managers who met countrywide sales and profitability goals would receive trips of their own. One of these trips was to Phoenix, Arizona, where we spent two days with an inspirational speaker followed by a visit to the Grand Canyon. Most of the directors had never been there before and were excited to see snow on the ground for the first time. It was a truly memorable trip.

Lilly/Dow-Elanco Brazil Board of Directors at the Grand Canyon, Arizona, spring 1989.

By the end of the decade, my sales, marketing, and manufacturing efforts for Elanco (our agricultural chemicals division of the company) underwent a massive change when Lilly sold it to Dow Chemical and then immediately entered into a joint-venture manufacturing services agreement with them. They named the new company Dow-Elanco, and I was responsible for overseeing the transfer of rights for the products and then their continued manufacturing.

All these initiatives combined to enable Lilly Brazil to increase our market share, get great prices for our products, protect our patents, and launch new products. Finally, we were making money.

Lilly Brazil wins the Top Growth prize in anti-infectives. L–R: Mr. Eugene Step (President of Lilly), me, and other Lilly executives. Indianapolis, Indiana, circa 1989.

Industry Leadership Roles

My work on intellectual property rights was very important and led me to become president of the Multinational Industry Association for Pharmaceuticals (Interfarma) in Brazil. I also became vice president of CIFAB (the Anglo-American Chamber of Pharmaceutical Industry) and participatd in the Sindusfarma and Abifarma pharmaceutical organizations.

In addition, I sat on the Committee on Foreign Investment in Brazil, which was part of the American Chamber of Commerce of São Paulo. This organization consisted of five or six representatives from foreign investment companies such as Citibank, General Motors, and, of course, Lilly. All the members were expatriates from the U.S. and Europe except for me; I was the only local Brazilian, which enabled me to help facilitate conversations about foreign investments in Brazil. I was also eventually nominated as an honorary life member of the American Chamber of Commerce of São Paulo due to my innovative intellectual property work within a U.S.-based company.

Environmental Protection

Toward the end of the decade, I initiated discussions to address the environmental waste caused by our manufacturing facility in Cosmopolis, located about one-and-a-half hours from São Paulo. In general, for every generated kilogram of a product, there may be twenty kilograms of accompanying waste, which is contaminated with toxic chemicals.

Back in the 1950s and 1960s, industrial companies around the world threw their waste into rivers or buried it underground. Both led to serious repercussions. Dumping the waste into the rivers immediately contaminated the surface waters and buried waste eventually leeched into the groundwater for miles and miles and miles.

Lilly did not want to do that.

After much discussion, we decided to build an incinerator to burn the waste rather than pay another company to properly dispose of it. I was tasked with obtaining the necessary approvals from the proper Brazilian authorities and overseeing its installation.

The incinerator cost the company a lot of money, but it was worth the investment. We were the first pharmaceutical company in Brazil to not only produce our products locally, but also safely and efficiently dispose of the resulting waste. In fact, the incinerator took care of not only our own product waste, but that of some other manufacturers as well.

Accepting other companies' waste turned out to be complicated, though. They were happy to pay us to properly dispose of their waste, but we were concerned about liability. If we accepted waste from them and something went awry during the incineration process, who would be responsible? And what would happen to the minuscule remaining waste? There's always something left over. It's like cremation; there are always some ashes, which are placed in an urn. So for our competitors, we established a legal framework, placed their residual waste into boxes, and returned it to them.

The incinerator operated weekdays on a regular nine-to-five work schedule; we weren't producing enough waste to operate it overnight. To prevent smoke and fumes or any kind of air contamination, we installed scrubbers. And we began to store our own residual waste deep underground in concrete-walled storage facilities to prevent access to any water source.

Industrialization leads to the creation of incredible new products, but it also generates unwanted waste that you have to get rid of. It's a real problem.

The new industrial incinerator for Dow-Elanco Brazil. Cosmopolis, S.P., Brazil, fall 1991.

Beyond Work

During our first four years in Brazil, Kathy and I lived in the Moema neighborhood of São Paulo near Parque Ibirapuera in the center of the city. Then, with my promotion to general manager, we moved to Chácara Santa Helena in the Santo Amaro section of the city.

My new position came with many responsibilities, which required a lot of hard work. I arrived at the office at six thirty on weekday mornings, often staying until seven or eight o'clock at night. Once home, I'd eat a late dinner, watch a little TV, and work for another hour or so before going to bed and starting the process all over again. Maintaining all this was intense, but that's the price we have to pay to be successful.

Nevertheless, I tried to reserve a little bit of the weekend to spend time with Kathy, who spent her week volunteering and, for a time, working as a substitute teacher at Graded American High School. We frequently visited my family who lived just three-and-a-half hours away in the interior of the state, and we regularly brought my mother, sisters, brothers, and all the nieces and nephews to tour the attractions in São Paulo.

Coincidentally or not, the 1980s was the decade when more than fifteen of my cousins got married. Kathy and I always received an invitation and many times, we were the ones who drove the bride to the church. We had our own private car as well as a company car, which we were allowed to use as we wished as long as we paid for its maintenance.

Each year, Kathy and I took a two-week vacation called a "home leave" to the U.S. In 1989, we brought my mother along with us to visit Kathy's parents in Pittsburgh and to see Lilly headquarters in Indianapolis. We also visited the Bells in Dimmitt, Texas, and concluded our trip at Disney World. Mom enjoyed every minute of the trip and considered it to be one of the most memorable events of her life, which, unbeknownst to us at the time, would soon change drastically.

Standing (L–R): Me, Kathy, Janice Bell, Lonnie Bell. Sitting: My mother, Dona Alzira. "AFSer Now Heads Eli Lilly & Co. in Brazil," *Castro County News*, Dimmitt, Texas, June 29, 1989.

Church remained important to both Kathy and me. When we lived outside the U.S., Kathy always went with me to the Catholic Church, where we made some great friends. Our other friends consisted of people from Lilly, our communities, the country club, the American Club,[34] and Kathy's numerous volunteer activities.

Despite our busy schedules, we always found time to do the things we wanted to do.

IMAGINATION AT ITS BEST

During my seven years in Brazil, I held three different managerial positions: director of marketing planning, director of operations, and general manager. Lilly's market ranking in pharmaceuticals changed from #22 in 1984 to #7 by 1989. Keflex®, which we manufactured locally, became the #1 pharmaceutical product in the entire Brazilian market—a major accomplishment for an affiliate of a multinational company.

Thanks to the talented executive team I relied on, we grew sales and market share, launched new products, engaged with the sales force to enhance motivation and accountability, and worked closely with the pricing folks.

Operations were restructured, distribution agreements were signed, incentive programs were implemented with great results, sales reached an all-time high, and Brazilian pharmaceuticals became profitable again. We shaped the external environment, and an incinerator was built to address the issue of waste generation and disposal in manufacturing.

---

34 A group for American expatriates with chapters in many countries of the world.

And in addition to all of this, we hired the first female into our sales force in 1986—a monumental event that ran contrary to everything the company had been doing up to that point. It was inconceivable that even though we had been in need of talented sales reps, we had not included more than 50 percent of the population in the employment pool. This policy change to ensure gender equality made our company attractive to many people who had previously seen discrimination as the norm.

The Big Picture

1980s Overview

WORLD / U.S. [35]

- Dow:[36] 838.74–2,753.20 +228%
- Planned economics move to laissez-faire
- Efforts made to relocate plants and other activities to developing countries like Mexico, Thailand, China, etc.
- Reagan scraps détente and moves more aggressively against Soviet Union
- Economic difficulties in many countries are helped by the International Monetary Fund and the World Bank
- IBM releases PC; Apple releases Macintosh in 1981
- Space shuttle lifts off
- Great advances in genetics and digital technology
- HIV becomes recognized (without cure) in 1980s
- Live Aid concert in 1985
- Two major disasters: Bhopal in 1984 and Chernobyl in 1986
- Emergence of terrorist organizations such as al-Qaeda
- Iraq-Iran war causes one million deaths
- Russia-Afghanistan conflict causes two million deaths
- Global Internet takes shape; "www" formalized in 1989
- Video game consoles like Atari 2600 become popular; Pac-Man becomes widespread

---

35 Source of historical data in this section: "1980s," Wikimedia Foundation, https://en.wikipedia.org/wiki/1980s. Last accessed September 26, 2023.

36 Source of the Dow range in this section: "Dow Jones Industrial Average," Wikimedia Foundation, https://en.wikipedia.org/wiki/Dow_Jones_Industrial_Average. Last accessed October 24, 2023.

- Gorbachev tries to reform communism with glasnost (political) and perestroika (economics); he fails
- Protests in Hungary and Tiananmen Square, Czechoslovakia has "Velvet Revolution," Romania's Ceauşescu is overthrown, the Berlin Wall falls, and Germany is reunified under Kohl—all in 1989

BRAZIL

- João Figueiredo, Tancredo Neves (never took office), José Sarney
- "Diretas Ja" pushes for redemocratization; succeeds in 1985
- Bresser Pereira (my former boss/professor at FGV) becomes Minister of Finance; launches "Bresser Plan" of economic stabilization
- External debt renegotiated through Brady bonds; "lost decade"

PERSONAL SIGNIFICANT EVENTS / ACHIEVEMENTS

- Lives in East Lansing, Michigan; Indianapolis, Indiana; Lubbock, Texas; Indianapolis, Indiana; Caracas, Venezuela; Santiago, Chile; São Paulo, Brazil
- Year of changes (new job, new car, new town, wife) in 1980
- Lilly International, Indianapolis (1980-1981)
- Lilly Venezuela, Caracas (1981-1982)
- Lilly Chile, Santiago (1982-1984)
- Lilly Brazil, São Paulo (1984-1991)

5

THE ARENA GOES GLOBAL

As we entered the 1990s, my position as general manager of Lilly/Dow-Elanco Brazil continued to keep me busy. Overseeing all three arms of the operation—pharmaceuticals, animal health, and agricultural chemicals—was not difficult from an accounting perspective, but it did require managing a lot of people.

Unable to oversee everything and everyone personally, I worked closely with an executive team consisting of a director of manufacturing, a government-affairs person, an HR director, a financial director, a medical director for pharmaceuticals, a director of pharmaceutical operations, a veterinarian to oversee animal health, and an agronomist for the agricultural chemicals. As I moved up the chain of command, I relied on these individuals even more heavily to ensure increased profitability.

There were three things I kept very tight control over. One was head count. On a weekly basis, I wanted to know how many people we had hired, how many we had fired, and how many employees had given notice or were nearing retirement. That was very important. The second thing was capital expenditures. Area managers could not build a factory or a building of any significance before I obtained approval from my boss. And the third thing was pricing. Lilly Brazil could not just introduce a product at any price; we had to follow the country's established global price guidelines. Convincing the government that we needed to increase our prices tended to be a long, drawn-out process, which led me to begin fighting hard for price freedom.

I was elated, therefore, when the Brazilian government finally lifted price controls in the early 1990s. Their hope was that it would entice more companies to hire more local people and build more manufacturing plants in Brazil.

Unfortunately, one of Lilly's competitors took advantage of the situation and increased their product prices 1,000 percent almost overnight. The general public who had to buy the drugs—many of whom didn't have insurance—simply couldn't afford the sudden, extreme price hikes. Within six months, the Brazilian government was forced to reimpose price controls.

The short-lived trial was deleterious to the pharmaceutical industry as a whole.

A CONVERSATION WITH THE U.S. PRESIDENT

In April 1990, U.S. President George H. W. Bush visited Brazil to push for intellectual property rights on a global scale through the development of a world trade organization. Since I served as president of CIFAB (the Anglo-American Chamber of Pharmaceutical Industry) and director of Abifarma (Brazilian Association of the Pharmaceutical Industry), I was invited to join the select number of executives who would meet the president at the American Embassy in Brasília.

Dr. Sartarelli greeting President George H. W. Bush at his reception at the American Embassy in Brasília, D.F., Brazil, fall 1990.

Upon my arrival, I joined the other guests in line for a brief one-on-one opportunity to greet the president. When it was my turn, I shook hands with President Bush and introduced myself as the general manager of Eli Lilly Brazil. His face lit up as he responded, "That's wonderful! I served as a director on Lilly's board for three years and was impressed by the company. How is Lilly doing in Brazil?"

I was pleased to reply, "Mr. President, Lilly Brazil is doing very well. We continue to work hard on intellectual property rights, and I hope we can continue to count on your support." That was the extent of our exchange before I had to move on.

Shortly afterward, Mario Amato, the president of Federação das Indústrias do Estado de São Paulo who had been standing in line behind me asked incredulously, "Sartarelli, how do you know this guy?" Just as astounded as he was about my exchange with the U.S. president, I informed him that I had never met him before.

President Bush's visit to Brazil helped the pharmaceutical industry tremendously; I believe it advanced the decision of future President Fernando Henrique Cardoso to recognize patents in 1996.

FIGHTING FOR PHARMACEUTICAL PATENT LAWS

A patent is important because it is a timed recognition of an invention. After the time period has elapsed—typically twenty years—it goes off patent and copies, often termed "generics," can be legally created. Patents also serve as an incentive for innovation, motivating scientists to discover new drugs. If their efforts aren't going to be recognized and protected, why would they bother devoting their careers to it? You have to protect patents; simple as that.

In the United States, unilateral patent laws have existed, uninterrupted, since the U.S. Constitution was ratified in 1788. Until recently, other countries have had patents for chemicals, foodstuffs, and all kinds of inventions, but not pharmaceuticals. They believed a proprietary patent should not be observed for pharmaceuticals because of their lifesaving benefits. It was ludicrous.

In addition, without a patent, cheaper copies will be made right away. The masses will then buy the generics instead of the brand-name drugs, causing the pharmaceutical companies to lose their investments. Not offering patents to protect all that makes no sense.

There's a misconception among the general public that pharmaceutical companies are just in it for the money and that they don't care about the people. But curing and managing disease is at the heart of all these companies do. It simply costs a lot of money to create new drugs and run clinical trials.

Consider the United States, whose federal government spends billions of dollars on innovation. The National Institutes of Health alone spends $50 billion on research and development every year. And pharmaceutical companies also spend billions of dollars of their own. For example, if I'm developing a product for blood pressure, I have to get it approved, which means I'll probably have to do a trial with twenty-five-thousand patients, which costs $50,000–$100,000 for each participant. Who pays for this? The pharmaceutical companies.

All told, it costs well over $1 billion dollars today to develop one new drug. It's mind-boggling. So in order to remain financially solvent and continue to create more new drugs, pharmaceutical companies have to recover their money by selling their drugs at a commensurate price for a protected amount of time, both at home and abroad.

HARD WORK LEADS TO NEW OPPORTUNITIES

After seven years at the helm of Lilly/Dow-Elanco Brazil, I was eager to try my hand at something new. Conversations ensued with my bosses and in 1991, I was promoted to director of international marketing planning under Robert Luedke, head of international marketing. This position would move Kathy and me back to Indianapolis, but before I could leave Brazil, my replacement had to be found.

Roy Cage was instrumental in persuading Dr. Richard Morrison to assume my position. Dr. Morrison, who had been serving as general manager of Lilly Mexico, was the ultimate internationalist, having worked and lived in many different places around the world.

In our short time together, I discovered he shared my passion for hard work. I had learned early in my career that not everyone shares this important quality. In fact, the biggest challenge I faced as general manager was employee procrastination. To ensure things get done on time or better yet, early, you have to take immediate action and put in the work required. Hard work is what propelled my career.

I confidently handed the reigns over to Dr. Morrison, knowing he was capable of taking Lilly/Dow-Elanco to new heights. Little did

I know then that we would work together again one day and become close friends.

I welcome the new General Manager of Lilly/Dow-Elanco Brazil, Dr. Richard Morrison (far right) with Kathy seated beside me (right). São Paulo, S.P., Brazil, fall 1991.

LILLY INTERNATIONAL

In the fall of 1991, Kathy and I left Brazil and bought our first house—a beautiful French-style, white-brick home with a garden—in the suburb of Carmel, north of Indianapolis, Indiana. Almost immediately we began to entertain family and friends; at one point we even hosted a family reunion for Kathy's Illinois relatives. Unfortunately, opportunities to entertain and host my own family were about to diminish significantly.

Our first home. Carmel, Indiana, fall 1991.

Soon after we arrived in Indianapolis, my American mother, Janice Bell, passed away on October 24, 1991. She had developed lupus a few years earlier and suffered greatly before succumbing to the disease. Her loss had a major impact on the Bells and on me; Janice had been instrumental in my coming to live with them as an AFS student in 1967.

Less than a year after losing Janice, I lost Alzira, my real mother, on August 16, 1992. Six months after her trip to the U.S. with us in 1989, she was diagnosed with oral cancer and underwent a successful surgery at the A.C. Camargo Cancer Center in São Paulo with a top specialist. It was also an invasive surgery, making it difficult for her to speak afterward. But she was strong and enjoyed remission for about eighteen months before the cancer returned twice. She died with her daughters by her side. I was on a business trip in South Korea and was unable to return in time for the funeral.[37]

For the first time in my life, I felt the weight of being an orphan, having now lost both my mother and my father. It took me many months to adjust.

Dona Alzira, my mother, in her mid to late sixties at home in Brazil.

37 Burial in Brazil is customarily performed twenty-four hours after death.

New Product Launches

There was much to do in my new position, especially since I was now launching products in 200 different countries. Aside from the European Union that approved or disapproved drugs unilaterally for all its twenty-or-so members, Lilly's products had to be launched in each country one by one.

I was in charge of preparing documentation and paperwork, approving marketing leaflets and pamphlets, and supporting the training of all our medical personnel and sales team members. It was a lot of work, but if you're launching a cardiovascular drug, HIV product, or a vaccine that can benefit millions of people, you're going to have to prepare your direct-marketing planning.

The hardest part is training your sales force. Convincing doctors to start using your product just by showing a bag full of promotional materials and maybe some samples is very hard to do. Even if you're successful at that initial sales call, it often takes six months to a year for the physician to actually start prescribing your product. The goal is to overcome their objections and get them to recommend it right away.

To help the sales team understand how doctors might respond, we hired several physicians to participate in mock sales pitches. A training session for when we launched Prozac® might have gone something like this:

"I know you're treating depression. You're probably prescribing amitriptyline—a load molecule that works very well but has all kinds of side effects. Would you consider this new drug?"

And the doctor might respond, "Well, it's too expensive."

"Actually, it's not expensive, it's reimbursed."

"Okay, fine. But does it work?"

"I'm going to give you a couple articles about our bona-fide, double-blind studies that prove it works. I just want you to try the product. If it doesn't work, stop using it. But if it does work, then you've got another option to treat depression."

In real life, too, we simply wanted to provide doctors with all the information and case studies and let them decide whether the product was right for their patients. If they opted not to use it, we'd simply thank them for their time and not think any less of them. But we wanted them to use it if it made sense for their patients.

Some drugs, of course, were accepted more readily than others. The drug we launched for multiple myeloma, for example, was much easier to sell because doctors are more willing to give a new drug a try if there's a chance it will save their patients' lives. Even if a drug can't cure certain diseases, it can often at least help manage the condition, like our drugs are doing for HIV and both type 1 and type 2 diabetes.

It should be noted that if salespeople offered physicians kickbacks or induced them in any way other than providing them with the approved marketing materials and samples, it was cause for immediate termination. We had zero tolerance for that—not just within Lilly, but among all the major pharmaceutical companies. Never, in any of the three pharmaceutical companies that I worked for, did I ever hear anything different from my boss or anyone up the corporate ladder. If anyone was caught bribing doctors—it didn't matter if he or she was a top salesperson, led district sales, or was a generally nice person—they were fired on the spot. Gone, gone, gone with no reprieve.

But that doesn't mean that an occasional physician didn't ask for something in return. One time when I spoke with a physician in Southeast Asia, he said, "You don't have to worry about me. I'll prescribe the products. Just give me $1,000 a month."

Shocked, I responded, "I'm going to pretend I didn't hear what you just said. But if you hold to what you said, I'm going to tell my sales rep to stop visiting you." The only thing we ever asked physicians to do was evaluate our products and use them at their medical discretion. We never wanted them to use the products because they were making money off them.

I was relentless about that on every continent I worked. It's critical to uphold medical ethics. The doctor's decision should be made by purely medical, not commercial, factors. It was that simple.

Planning and Repurposing

Many times when pharmaceutical companies were launching new products, they stopped thinking about existing ones and missed out on sales opportunities. Thus, in an effort to optimize our existing products, I reintroduced the "life cycle planning" process.

In essence, "life cycle planning" is looking at the product through the lens of multiple indications over time. For example, Prozac® was great for treating depression as well as anxiety. However, each of these indications required one to three clinical trials to prove its effectiveness. Since the opportunity was so big in depression, the company decided to launch it only for depression, not for the other indication.

However, if all the clinical trials for each indication are done at the outset, it allows companies to launch one product for several indications at once, which is what we did with a multimillion-dollar biologic product used for Crohn's disease, eczema, and osteoporosis. But even after drugs have already been on the market, companies can sometimes still go back and breathe new life into them by initiating clinical trials and obtaining the necessary approvals to sell the drugs to a different demographic. It all depends on how much time is still left on the patent.

Patent filing and regulatory approval are both required for a new drug and must be done separately. From the patent standpoint, if you have an idea that your drug might work for multiple indications and you meet the scientific filing requirements, you should file for as many indications as you can as early as possible since the approval process takes several years. During that time, they check to see whether there's an existing similar product on the market or if another company has filed for a new but similar product patent before you. It's a competitive filing process. Once you've been approved, the patent covers your drug for the indications you listed for twenty years unless you file for an extension.

So you may end up with patents for multiple health issues, but then you have to prove that the drug works by successfully completing clinical trials and receiving regulatory approval before you can market and sell the drug. Your research-and-development department has to be very good to quickly prove to the federal government that this works for the indication in question. The sooner you do it, the more patent life you have.

So as I considered the life cycle of the products, I had to look at it from a commercial perspective. I didn't want to develop a clinical trial for a drug and be ready to launch it, but then not have a patent to protect it. In addition, I had to keep in mind the patent expiration dates for our existing drugs that might be useful for other indications. There was no point initiating a ten-year clinical trial for an indication with a drug that has a patent that expires in less than eight years. In the end, I created a list of five to ten products that were included in the life-cycle process, which led to many extra years of sales for each of them.

The only time a lengthy clinical trial has been waived was during the COVID-19 pandemic. In an effort to get a vaccine out as quickly as possible, the government approved both Moderna's and Pfizer's vaccines based on small clinical trials that lasted less than one year. Since they seemed to work, they were launched. Such a short approval process had never happened before and hasn't happened again.

New Horizons

As much as I appreciated my staff position in international marketing planning, I nevertheless missed the operational side. The ability to restore an organization to profitability is exciting because there's so much to be done. And it's difficult, which also makes it a lot more fun. I loved the operational side and let my superiors know my preference when discussing the next stage of my career.

Late in 1992, Roy Cage offered me the opportunity to build a presence for Lilly in the Asia-Pacific market—an exciting new hemisphere for me. Kathy and I had only lived in Indianapolis for about a year and had anticipated several more years in the States, but when once-in-a-lifetime opportunities arise, you take them. I accepted the offer with the agreement that we would not move before Kathy's birthday on February 14, 1993, so she could celebrate with her family.

LILLY ASIA PACIFIC

Kathy and I arrived in Singapore in April 1993. For the first two months, we lived at the Shangri-La Singapore, a hotel advertised as "a tropical sanctuary in the heart of the city," until our container ship arrived with our furnishings. We always shipped all our possessions, including books and furniture, to each country we lived in—and added more along the way.

Within days I was comfortable driving on the left side of the road, commuting between the hotel on Orange Grove Road and Lilly's office on Orchard Boulevard at the Forum Complex. There were very strict rules to be obeyed in Singapore, such as no jaywalking, which made it an orderly, safe place to live.

As the area director of Asia Pacific, my job was to grow Lilly's business in South Korea, China, Taiwan, Hong Kong, Thailand, Vietnam, the Philippines, India, Malaysia, Singapore, Indonesia, Australia, and New Zealand plus Sri Lanka, Nepal, Myanmar, Laos, Cambodia, Bangladesh, and the Pacific Islands. Four of those countries—China, India, Vietnam, and Indonesia—required special attention because of their large market sizes and the fact that we had not yet established a presence there. We continued to use distributors from Thailand and Australia to extend our reach to the smallest markets.

China and India were the target of many of my business trips each year, where I engaged directly with authorities to ensure intellectual property rights were respected, prices were as free as possible, and regulatory affairs were running efficiently and effectively as we entered the markets there. My team and I also traveled two or three times a year to our two biggest and well-established operations: South Korea and Australia. And in 1994, when Randy Tobias became Lilly's CEO, the two of us traveled together to China, the Philippines, Australia, and India to meet with the prime ministers and presidents of various countries.

Lilly CEO/Chairman Randy Tobias visits with the President of the
Philippines, Fidel Ramos, as I look on (far right).
Manila, Philippines, fall 1994.

I was highly engaged within the company, within the industry, and among the local governments in the countries in which I worked. I also stayed abreast of what was happening back in my native Brazil.

Shortly after Fernando Henrique Cardoso was elected president of Brazil in 1994, he launched the real currency plan. Prior to that, we used the cruzeiro in the 1940s–1980s, which was named after the Southern Cross constellation visible only in the Southern Hemisphere. This was followed by the cruzado, and then the real, which remains Brazil's currency today.

Brazilians were eager to have a stable currency after years of inflation, devaluation, and high interest rates. People had to save money and buy in cash; they just could not afford a mortgage. So a lot of people welcomed the new real that came out in 1994. It significantly reduced inflation over the years to what is currently a nominal, very acceptable rate. It was the best thing that could ever have happened to the Brazilian people and enabled the country to finally start feeling normal again.

Entering New Markets

Roy Cage retired in 1993 and was replaced by Sidney Taurel as executive vice president and president of pharmaceuticals worldwide. Sidney indicated that he did not expect me to lose more than $10 million a year while setting up a presence in China. I love a challenge, so I immediately committed to that goal.

My first order of business was to establish a joint-venture partnership with an existing Chinese company—a requirement of the Chinese government. My team and I identified a potential partner in the city of Suzhou, a big city outside of Shanghai. The problem, however, was that when we initiated shareholding discussions, we learned they didn't know exactly who owned the company since they were formed as a department of a university or attached to the state government. I refused to sign a contract for a joint venture until I knew exactly whom I was going to be working with, which took approximately six months to sort out.

In 1994, we finally established the Lilly Suzhou joint venture with a 90 percent Lilly/10 percent Suzhou company split. It was a hard-won share agreement that required much effort, focus, and negotiations. Happy with the financials, we conceded that they could create additional joint-venture partnerships with other companies in noncompeting industries. I traveled from Singapore to China literally every month until we got the operation up and running.

Lilly Suzhou Pharmaceutical Company Ltd.'s joint-venture signing ceremony (I'm seated at the table on the far left), fall 1994.

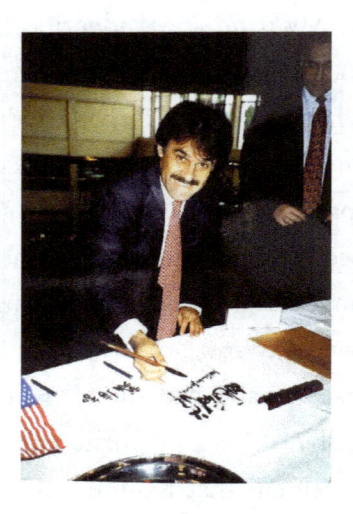

I smile as I sign the paperwork to begin working with our partner in Suzhou, China, fall 1994.

There were several other things we had to do in China during that time as well: determine whether to locate or build a manufacturing plant; register our top-selling products; build an operations team comprised of HR, marketing, and finance experts; and gather a well-trained sales force. My team in Singapore oversaw most of those functions, but we needed an expert to oversee regulatory affairs. That individual was Dr. Margaret Hsu, a consultant based in

Princeton who spoke many languages and, most importantly, knew many people at the Chinese Ministry of Health. She was a pleasure to work with and was instrumental to our successful entrance into the Middle Kingdom.

L-R: I stand beside Lilly's CEO/Chairman, Randy Tobias (center), at his arrival in Beijing, China, fall 1994.

I visited the Great Wall of China with Sidney Taurel (black coat) and two members of our Suzhou joint-venture partner company. Mid-1990s.

The role of the local joint-venture company was to handle all registrations and ensure payment to the government. Our local Chinese partner really helped us in many ways. For example, if we had a problem with the minister of health, the partner would accompany us to the meetings and speak on our behalf. They were in charge of registrations and relationships with the state and federal governments while we took care of sales and manufacturing.

China, unlike Brazil, didn't have to borrow from Bank of America or Citibank or any financial institution to fund their development. Rather, they created the conditions (export-driven economy) and made it attractive for international companies to establish and maintain operations in their country. For example, we entered China at the same time as General Motors. The only difference between our entrances was that Lilly invested one-fortieth of what General Motors brought in. The amounts of foreign investments that continue to flow directly into China are huge.

During this same time, we were also setting up operations in Vietnam and Indonesia, where we were negotiating with Tempo, a local company that had a successful history of hosting foreign companies and products. In addition, we were overseeing the new Lilly-Ranbaxy joint venture in New Delhi, India. Ranbaxy Laboratories was the #1 pharmaceutical company in India at the time.

A ceremony celebrating the launch of the Lilly-Ranbaxy joint venture was held outdoors in New Delhi at the historic ruins of the Mughal emperor. Flower petals formed decorations on the ground and a feast was served including chai tea, which Kathy and I tasted for the first time. During another trip, the general manager of Lilly India, Andrew Mascarenhas, and his family treated Kathy and me to an incredible visit to the Taj Mahal. Along the way we stopped at Bharatpur Bird Sanctuary (now known as Keoladeo National Park) where we enjoyed bicycling around the beautiful landscape.

At every country I visited, the local affiliate took very good care of my Singapore office team. We had many opportunities to enjoy the cuisine and sights of such colorful capital cities as Sydney, Auckland, Seoul, Bangkok, Shanghai, Beijing, and New Delhi. Other memorable meeting locations were at Langkawi, Malaysia, and the Shangri-La hotels in Kota Kinabalu, Malaysia, and Cebu, Philippines.

All told, China, India, Vietnam, and Indonesia took a lot of our time, but it was necessary work that enabled Lilly to grow by double digits after we launched many new products. Occasional faux pas were made along the way, but they were learning experiences.

The Intercultural Workplace

If you become a global company in the modern world, you're going to have to manage various cultural differences. My general managers in Thailand, Australia, South Korea, and India were all local hires within their respective countries, but at one point we also had a Singaporean running China and a Colombian running the Philippines operation. Although all of them spoke English, their cultural practices varied widely. Being mindful of these differences was important when dealing with our customers as well.

Consider payments, for example. Receivables are not a problem in the U.S. but are in many other countries—even the rich ones. It was not uncommon for clients to buy our pharmaceuticals, receive them, and use them but not pay for two years. By the time they got around to paying, they would then ask for a discount. It was ridiculous. They used our products, a number of their patients got better, and then they didn't want to pay a fair price. It was a very unfortunate situation.

By and large, however, I enjoyed my job. I wasn't required to entertain much; treating people in a respectful fashion and making a personal visit to their offices was typically enough. I did, however, frequently travel with Lilly's chairman to visit the presidents and prime ministers of the countries in which we were operating. These influential individuals were generally happy to meet with us because they knew if a CEO was coming in, investment was forthcoming. We were able to secure these meetings through the help of our local operations representatives, the U.S. Consular Office, and outside consultants.

My travel also included checking on the operations in each of the countries I managed, attending industry-wide meetings in different parts of the world, and making visits to Lilly headquarters in the U.S. at least six times a year. Every trip from Singapore to Indianapolis was twenty-five thousand miles. I was literally going around the earth six times a year for those meetings alone. Throughout my entire pharmaceutical career, I accumulated an incredible amount of flight miles with each of the major airlines: 2.5+ million miles with Northwestern (which is now Delta), 2.5+ million on Continental/United, and another 700,000 on American. That's a lot of travel.

Whenever possible, I took Kathy along on my business trips at our own expense, which provided her an opportunity to get to know the countries near Singapore, and we also took home-leave trips to visit her family in the United States and mine in Brazil. Plus, as in my previous positions, I rewarded my staff and employees with trips. My team of expats and local hires in Singapore worked extremely well together and so once a year, we went on an employee-plus-family weekend trip to such resort destinations as Phuket, Thailand, and the beautiful island of Bintan, Indonesia.

The Sartarelli siblings at Luzia's home. L–R: Tilim, Carlito, Cidinha, Luzia, and me. São Carlos, S.P., Brazil, mid-1990s.

ESTABLISHMENT OF THE WORLD TRADE ORGANIZATION (WTO)

Before the World Trade Organization (WTO) was established in 1995, international governments hosted eight different tariff and trade conferences between 1947 and 1994 to discuss the rights and regulations associated with selling goods, products, and services internationally. Yet, incredibly, none of those trade talks included intellectual property rights.

Thus, when the WTO adopted TRIPS (Trade-Related Aspects of Intellectual Property Rights), those of us in the industry rejoiced. All countries were required to amend their laws to honor intellectual property, including pharmaceutical patents. China had anticipated the move and was proactive, honoring intellectual property rights in 1993, two years before the WTO was established. Brazil incorporated the patent law in 1996.[38] Most of Europe also adopted it in

---

38 Throughout my work with the pharmaceutical industry and many governments, I sought to encourage and motivate authorities to recognize patents for pharmaceuticals. In 1994, Lilly and the industry published a summary of our efforts in Brazil: "Patentes para produtos farmacêuticos: Mudando paradigmas, moderizando o Brasil" ("Patents for pharmaceutical products: Shifting paradigms, modernizing Brazil").

a timely manner. But India claimed financial hardships and received a ten-year extension. It's my understanding they still haven't fully amended their policies.

An interesting side effect of the WTO was that a lot of companies stopped manufacturing overseas and resumed exporting to key markets. It's completed a full circle: From the 1950s to 1970s, countries mostly imported everything. Then between the 1980s and 2000s, they opened up to a lot of international manufacturing to supply their local markets. And now more recently, a lot of those plants have either been closed or sold and the countries are back to importing. Take China, for example. It's my understanding that Lilly sold their manufacturing plant—the one I helped establish—some time ago to a Chinese company. I assume China now imports Lilly's products.

It all comes down to the politics of the moment.

Home Life

With limited English-language TV offerings in Singapore, Kathy and I typically watched CNN in the morning and listened to the BBC on the radio throughout the day. We rented videos (Westerns continued to be my favorite) from Mr. O'Dell's store and enjoyed exploring the multicultural city of Singapore, which was filled with colonial and World War II history. It was a tropical paradise with lush gardens and an equatorial climate. We enjoyed every minute we were there.

Kathy's sister Susie came to visit annually, often at Thanksgiving to help cook a turkey and meet the friends we invited to share our holiday meal. We became close friends with a small group of Brazilians who were fellow expats far from home, and we attended a special wedding when our finance director married a Singaporean.

Kathy and I also took vacations to such places as the Forbidden City, the Great Wall of China, historic palaces in Seoul and Bangkok, and temples in Bali. We also traveled to Australia to see Uluru /Ayers Rock and the Great Barrier Reef, being sure to visit my former boss, Don Joyce, who had retired to the land Down Under, and his family.

Uluru/Ayers Rock—a mountain in the center of Australia's desert that is considered sacred ground to the Aboriginal people. Alice Springs, Australia, early 1990s.

Don Joyce (far left) and his family, whom Kathy and I visited in Australia after his retirement from Lilly. Sydney, Australia, 1997.

Turning Point

By 1997, Lilly Asia Pacific was financially stable, had acquired significant market share in many places, and its new operations in China and India were picking up speed. In South Korea, we had even bought out our joint-venture partner and anticipated accelerated growth throughout the region.

It was during this time that I was approached by Quinton Oswald, an executive from Bristol-Myers Squibb (BMS), at a pharmaceutical meeting in Phuket, Thailand. He was impressed by the things I was doing in Asia Pacific and felt I should get to know his company. He mentioned there were some young executives at BMS with great potential I should get to know and suggested I travel to the U.S. to talk to them about a job.

The conversation was fortuitous as I had been requesting an advancement within Lilly to no avail. In addition, Kathy had been growing increasingly concerned about living so far away from her aging parents. We both wanted to spend more time with them while they were still healthy and active in their retirement.

Once again I went to Sidney Taurel, the president of Lilly, who again assured me they were looking for something for me, but nothing was immediately available. I decided it was time to pursue the BMS opportunity.

BRISTOL-MYERS SQUIBB

Bristol-Myers Squibb was formed when two different pharmaceutical companies merged, effectively bringing many talented scientists and executives together at its main site in Lawrenceville, New Jersey, near Princeton. I flew there to meet the BMS executives I had been told about—Don Hayden Jr., who was the president of the intercontinental region, and Christine "Chris" Poon, who oversaw medical devices. They made me an offer at double my salary that I was happy to accept.

I was eager to assume my new position, but I first had to return to Singapore to finalize a few things. As I was preparing for the transition, the Asian financial crisis hit. What started in Thailand quickly spread to East and Southeast Asia, causing much money confusion. It forced a correction that negatively affected not only the countries themselves, but the foreign companies doing business in those countries as well. The economy was eventually stabilized through the International Monetary Fund, which stepped in to provide rescue money.

On July 18, 1997, I officially resigned from Eli Lilly and Company. The departure from Lilly after almost seventeen years of employment was difficult and heart-wrenching. It was, after all, the company that had made me an international executive, taught me the fundamentals of my professional life, and enabled me to form multiple friendships in Indianapolis, Latin America, and throughout the Asia-Pacific region. Yet Kathy and I were equally excited about our future as we moved into our new home in Hopewell, New Jersey.

Our second home. Hopewell, New Jersey, late 1990s.

My new role as senior vice president, franchise management, intercontinental region was a staff position in which I provided marketing leadership and support to all BMS operations in Canada,

Latin America, Africa, the Middle East, and Asia Pacific. I was involved in marketing planning, marketing research, support for sales training in the affiliates, strategic planning, and HR management (particularly succession planning).

Another key responsibility of my position was portfolio development, which involved prioritizing our vast list of patented products across the entire intercontinental region. The only areas *not* in my purview were the U.S. and Western Europe, which combined only comprised about 20 percent of the world in terms of geography. This meant that I was responsible for getting our products into the remaining three-quarters of the world. Needless to say, identifying which drugs to prioritize in each country was very time-consuming.

I could not market products unilaterally because the products driving sales growth in Japan were different from the products driving sales in Brazil, just as the drug needs in the UK were different from those in France. Plus, I had to factor in each country's economic situation. In Nicaragua, for example, the maximum that I was ever going to sell was $500,000 a year whereas in Japan, I could sell $100 million multiple times per year.

On top of that, I had to wait for approval from each country before launching each product. The UK and Australia required a local clinical trial before approving a drug, but the other countries, back in those days, did not require their own clinical trials. If you had the product approved in the U.S., UK, or Australia, the other countries would accept your product documentation based on the quality of those registrations.

Prioritizing countries and products were critical challenges within franchise management.

Job Promotion

In January 1998, I was promoted to president of Asia Pacific, Japan, Middle East, and Africa. Within a mere six months, I went from overseeing $200 million in pharmaceutical sales with Lilly to $1.5 billion in sales of both pharmaceuticals and consumer medicines with BMS. The position was a wonderful challenge and provided me with an operational job of the greatest magnitude.

I continued to be based out of Princeton but traveled like crazy. Because I was expected to deliver double-digit growth of sales and profits while ensuring compliance along the way, I visited all my major countries to review their budgets and learn what they were intending to do the following year in terms of product launches and sales. Approving their budgets was very, very time-consuming and tons of work.

To assist me in my day-to-day efforts, I had three international vice presidents reporting to me. One was in Paris and in charge of most of Africa, another was in Cairo and oversaw the Middle East and East Africa, and the third was based in Singapore and was responsible for Asia Pacific. I also had a president in Japan overseeing that singularly huge market. With me in Princeton, I had a terrific team comprised of the heads of marketing, regulatory affairs, medical, government affairs, finance, and HR.

Despite my busy schedule, I also began to work more closely with the Pharmaceutical Research and Manufacturers of America (PhRMA) and some of its committees. Between 1998 and 2000, the industry elected me chairman of the PhRMA Asia-Pacific Committee and subsequently chair of many other committees.

My direct reports for Asia Pacific, Japan, Middle East, and Africa. I'm in the center wearing the red shirt. Princeton, New Jersey, spring 1998.

Upholding Mandates

One day as I was preparing to fly back to the U.S. from Japan, I received a call from Chris Poon, who had become president of international. She had heard from the competent chief financial officer in Turkey that compliance had been compromised and needed to be reestablished.

Since Turkey was part of my territory, I switched flights and flew to Istanbul to begin meeting with employees to determine what had happened. The courage demonstrated by the CFO was amazing. I was struck by her willingness to whistle-blow on her organization with such thoroughness and candor.

What I learned was that the general manager had done very well for five years, building the operation from zero sales to multimillion dollars. But then this individual and his team created an incentive program for the physicians in which the top prescribers would receive a color-TV set. By the time we learned about it, approximately one thousand TVs had been given to physicians all over the country.

Of course, that was not permitted at all; compliance was very important to us, and we went at the incentive program with a vengeance, dismissing the general manager and approximately 200 sales reps. Even though we replaced everyone within six months, it nevertheless crippled our sales for a couple of years as we reestablished physician relationships. In the meantime, we relied heavily on our distributors in Turkey to sell to pharmacies.

I also had to rectify the other mistake of undercapitalization. Because Turkey had a hyperinflationary economy and our loans were not adjusted accordingly, we were making zero profit as our debts continued to pile up. I had to bring in real money to pay off our loans, which then allowed us to start making a profit.

These experiences in Turkey and elsewhere taught us much about courage, financial integrity, and compliance. They also reaffirmed to me that the five mandates I had developed in my work at Lilly remained fully applicable and appropriate anywhere one wished to succeed in the long term:

- Do not ever lie
- Do not bribe people
- Do not break ethical standards
- Do not harass people, either physically or mentally
- Do not utilize funky accounting

Flying on the Concorde

In 1997, my boss and I had a layover in London while returning from a meeting in Cairo. As we were waiting for our connecting flight back to the U.S., he looked at his watch and sighed.

He said, "Zito, it's twelve o'clock now and we still face an eight-hour flight home. Couldn't we do it faster?"

"The only way to go faster is to take the Concorde," I replied.

"Let's do it."

The Concorde was known for flying at two times the speed of sound (Mach 2), which equates to about one thousand four hundred miles per hour. It held about one hundred people, was very long, and beautiful.

It also flew at 58,000 feet. Most commercial flights top out at 35,000–40,000 feet max. We were so high up that when we looked outside, we could see the curvature of the earth. Crazy! And the walls were very hot to the touch—the plane was very narrow, with only one seat on each side of the aisle, giving everyone a window seat.

Our flight-of-a-lifetime lasted a mere three hours and twenty minutes. Before exiting the plane, we got to visit the cockpit and the captain handed us a certificate to commemorate the trip. Just a few years later, the Concorde was grounded forever for financial reasons.

Concorde flight certificate commemorating my flight from London to New York on November 7, 1997.

Preparing for the End - Y2K

By late 1999, concerns about the dawning of the new millennium with the year 2000 (aka Y2K) had reached fever pitch. News outlets everywhere warned of possible mass technology failure on a global scale at the stroke of midnight on January 1, 2000, because computers had only been programmed to recognize years by their last two digits. Would computer chips incorrectly interpret the new "00" as a previous century instead of the new one? Everyone was scrambling to back up their data and prepare for the worst-case scenario.

BMS gave each member of upper management a gigantic cell-phone-like device with a little antenna, which I was instructed to take with me to Brazil, where Kathy and I were going to celebrate Christmas and New Year's. If the computers and traditional cell phones failed because of Y2K, I was to point the antenna of the device toward the satellite. The IT department, who was on standby and had the coordinates for the satellites, would then be able to connect me with the rest of the leadership team.

I never used it. No one used it. The clock struck twelve and technology everywhere still worked. The consulting companies should have been held responsible for all the anxiety they promoted and used to earn fortunes. It was just ridiculous. A lot of stuff was developed and oversold for an event that never happened. It was the biggest hoax ever.

IMAGINATION AT ITS BEST

The arena had indeed gone global. The 1990s saw me advancing through five positions with two companies, working in multiple countries and different hemispheres. I experienced a variety of company and societal cultures as I worked in the U.S., Latin America, Asia Pacific, the Middle East, and Africa.

Successfully managing businesses in difficult financial situations was a unique qualification that I upheld throughout my career. I was one of the few Latin Americans to do so in two completely different business environments (Latin America and Asia Pacific/Japan). In addition, once I was back in the U.S., I became more engaged with PhRMA and its efforts on behalf of the pharmaceutical industry. In the early 1990s, I was engaged with industry in Brazil (CIFAB, Interfarma, Abifarma), and subsequently with industry in Singapore, Southeast Asia, and China, and then international PhRMA.

I was enjoying every minute of my global career. I had joined Lilly in 1980 with the goals of working in marketing, working for a company with a presence in Brazil, and working internationally. All three things came to fruition … and imagination played a vital role in all of it.

The Big Picture

1990s Overview

WORLD / U. S. [39]

- Dow:[40] 2,753.20–11,497.12, +318%
- End of Cold War and beginning of the War on Terrorism
- *Hubble* repair launches into space in 1991
- Boris Yeltsin dissolves the Soviet Union in 1991
- Gulf War begins in 1991
- Multiculturalism engulfs the U.S.
- Grunge, Eurodance, and hip-hop music become popular
- Advances in www, gene therapy, cloning
- Oslo Accords signed in 1993
- Dolly the sheep becomes the first mammal to be cloned
- Rwandan genocide, 1994
- Dot-com frenzy leads to dot-com bubble of 1997–2000
- www gains a public face
- New conflicts in the Balkans and the Caucasus
- The Troubles in Northern Ireland come to a standstill in 1998
- Princess Diana dies in 1997

BRAZIL

- José Sarney, Fernando Collor de Mello, Itamar Franco, Fernando Henrique Cardoso

---

39 Source of historical data in this section: "1990s," Wikimedia Foundation, https://en.wikipedia.org/wiki/1990s. Last accessed September 26, 2023.

40 Source of the Dow range in this section: "Dow Jones Industrial Average," Wikimedia Foundation, https://en.wikipedia.org/wiki/Dow_Jones_Industrial_Average. Last accessed October 24, 2023.

- Redemocratization continues
- Patent Law is approved in 1996
- Brazil wins the soccer World Cup in Los Angeles in 1994

PERSONAL SIGNIFICANT EVENTS / ACHIEVEMENTS

- Lives in São Paulo, Brazil; Indianapolis, Indiana; Singapore; Hopewell/Princeton, New Jersey
- Lilly Brazil, São Paulo (1990–1991)
- President, CIFAB (1990–1991)
- President, Interfarma (1991)
- Director, Abifarma (1990–1991)
- Honorary Life Member of American Chamber of Commerce, São Paulo (1991)
- Lilly International, Indianapolis (1991–1993)
- Lilly Asia Pacific, Singapore (1993–1997)
- Member of Singapore American Chamber of Commerce (1994–1997)
- Engages with Industry in Southeast Asia/works closely with PhRMA in the U.S.
- Bristol-Myers Squibb (BMS), Princeton (1997–2000)
- Chair of PhRMA Asia Pacific Committee (1998–2000)

LOSSES

- Janice Bell, "American mother," October 24, 1991
- Mother, Alzira, August 16, 1992

6

DOING WELL BY DOING GOOD

BRISTOL-MYERS SQUIBB

In early 2000, I was asked to fill the newly vacated position of president of Latin America, Puerto Rico, and Canada; as in my previous positions, I would be based out of New Jersey and travel regularly. I accepted the offer and immediately faced a major currency devaluation in Brazil—our largest market in the region—which initiated a three-year recession. Devaluation was always a problem in Brazil. The only solution for a company was to sell more, but our #1 product there started to face tough generic competition at the same time.

In light of this, I had to restage Brazil, Mexico, and Canada in order to reach our goal of double-digit growth in sales and profitability. The other company executives and I believed that a relaunch of Pravachol® and the eventual introduction of Taxol® would put us back in the game.

BMS Mexico meeting. L-R: Stephen Cobham (President of BMS Mexico), Julio Frenk Jr. (Minister of Health of Mexico, currently the President of the University of Miami), Rick Lane (President of BMS Worldwide Pharmaceuticals), and me.

Shortly after I had taken over the position, Chris Poon, president of BMS International, and I met with Rick Lane, our new boss who had replaced Don Hayden Jr. as president of worldwide pharmaceuticals. I gave an update about my regions and concluded by stating the numbers we had hoped to reach could not be met because of the Brazilian devaluation.

Rick got upset and went on and on until Chris stood up and said, "Rick, I think Zito's doing a wonderful job trying to fix something we wanted him to fix. It makes no sense to pester him. I'm the president of international. If you have a problem with the numbers, you should pester me, but whether I'm going to take it or not, that's a different story." He turned bright red, and she walked out of the room.

In retrospect, I believe she had already committed to go somewhere else because a week or so later, she left BMS to become worldwide chairman of pharmaceuticals at Johnson & Johnson.

I continued in my position, frequently traveling to Brazil and Mexico to check on our operations there. Since it was not uncommon at that time for U.S. executives to be kidnapped for ransom throughout Latin America, BMS, like many other U.S.-based companies, hired bodyguards for their managers in that region. During my visits, a security car led the way, a bodyguard rode in my car, and another security car followed behind.

The bodyguards took their jobs seriously. One time, I decided to visit the Sanctuary of Our Lady of Aparecida in Brazil, the second-largest cathedral in the world, after St. Peter's Basilica in the Vatican. While there, I went into the bathroom and was shadowed by two of the guards, who positioned themselves directly behind me. I had to instruct them to wait in the hallway until I came out.

Shaping the External Environment
When PhRMA (the Pharmaceutical Research and Manufacturers of America) made me chair of the PhRMA Asia Pacific Committee back in 1998 while I was president of BMS Asia Pacific, Middle East, and Africa, it gave me the opportunity to become highly engaged in intellectual property rights, pricing, and regulatory affairs—issues that were top of mind for every executive in the industry. PhRMA continued to take a lot of my time in the early 2000s, particularly once I became chair of the Canada Steering Committee (2000–2001) and chair of the Latin America Steering Committee (2001–2002).

These positions allowed me to help shape the external environment in ways that benefited the entire industry. For example, when I served as president of the Anglo-American Pharmaceutical Industry (CIFAB) in Brazil, I wasn't just representing Eli Lilly; I was also supporting Pfizer, Johnson & Johnson, BMS, Glaxo, Sanofi, and a bunch of other pharmaceutical companies around the world. They say there's power in numbers, and I believe that worked to our advantage.

For example, if a country was taking two years or more to register a product, I, as president of the group, would meet with the minister of health. "Look, we have a lot of products that have already launched in the U.S. but are still waiting to get registered here. What can you do to accelerate the launch of these products in your country?"

In the United States, pharmaceutical companies pay the FDA to get their products registered. The government still registers them at their own pace, but if a company doesn't pay, they'll never get anything approved. Hindering the process even more is that people change positions and laws are rewritten all the time, so the registrations often get overlooked. To offset this, I consistently tried to encourage efficiency and implementation within the regulatory departments.

The same was true for foreign pricing authorities. The U.S. didn't have price controls, but in Brazil, approximately fifty government workers constantly regulated pricing. So I took the time to get to know these people. I visited them frequently and always justified my requests with hard data. They didn't want to merely take my word for it; they wanted to see supporting documentation. Thanks to the rigorous U.S. documentation standards that we had already met, I was able to provide them with adequate documentation to validate why bringing in the thirty-fifth antibiotic for the same indication made sense.

When we sent registration material to the FDA in the U.S., we had to send boxes and boxes and boxes of documentation; it's like a whole room filled with paper. Do you think they bothered to read all that stuff? No, they didn't. They simply read the substantive summary or the preamble. Why read ten thousand pages when it's all encapsulated in a fifty-page summary?

Was providing all that extra documentation a stupid and inefficient process? Yes. But we continued to send so much paper to the FDA because if they happened to question something in the summary, we had to come in, go to those boxes, and pull out a corresponding document to support our claim. If it was not backed up in the files, we had a problem. Today, most of the documentation is provided electronically, which makes it much simpler. But if a question is asked that is not included in the summaries, the company still has to produce a documented answer.

It's not always smooth sailing after a company receives approval, though. Sometimes problems crop up with existing products, which is what happened with a BMS partner in India. They had three different factories: one for the highly regulated market, one for the semiregulated market, and one for nonregulated market. Each factory produced the same pharmaceutical products, just different excipients or strength levels.

On one occasion, the company inadvertently sent products from the nonregulated market to the highly regulated U.S. market. When the FDA tested the products and discovered the difference, they banned the products for ten years. It wasn't just two or three products; it was thirty products that could no longer enter the U.S.—our biggest market. Needless to say, additional quality-control measures were put in place to prevent a repeat occurrence.

Patent law was another area I focused on in my various chair positions within PhRMA. When patents for pharmaceuticals expire, generics enter the market, which sometimes requires temporary sublicense negotiations. That is part of influencing the external environment as well.

All these experiences reiterated the need for business professionals to follow three basic yet fundamental principles: (1) above all, one has to be truthful, (2) one has to play by the book, and (3) one has to work exceptionally hard to keep up with change. In our industry, staying up-to-date with all the regulatory changes was a job of its own.

I worked hard in my various leadership positions because I believed it was important to fight for price freedom, efficient regulatory affairs, and patent laws, all of which greatly affect pharmaceutical sales and patient outcomes.

Company Shakeup

At the end of 2001 and into 2002, BMS was charged with channel stuffing a product that was about to go generic. "Stuffing the channel" means you push a certain amount of a product into the market, creating an illusion of stability and growth so that investors continue to buy shares of that company. So whatever BMS told Wall Street regarding this particular drug was not correct. This serious lack of fiduciary responsibility misled the market, causing people to lose their investments.

It also led to financial losses for our product distributors. When a patent expires and a drug goes generic, its sale price lowers dramatically due to competition. This means distributors aren't able to recoup their investments, and therefore, pharmaceutical companies are expected to reimburse the distributors the difference between their original purchase price and the new sales price for however much of the product remains in their inventory. So when BMS communicated incorrect numbers to Wall Street, they also eliminated the need to reimburse distributors.

Their actions went against everything I stood for. I had known nothing about it, and I certainly didn't want to be associated with it. It was time to look for another job.

A Timely Opportunity

Coincidentally, that was when Chris Poon reached out to me about a position at Johnson & Johnson. When she left BMS, she had signed a noncompete clause that prevented her from recruiting or hiring anyone from BMS for twelve months. As soon as that time period drew to a close, she wasted no time in asking me to help her grow Johnson & Johnson. It was an exciting offer since J&J was a much bigger company than any of my previous employers, a fact that remains true today. Eli Lilly is currently a $30 billion company and BMS is a $46 billion company, but J&J is almost an $100 billion company. It's the biggest and most successful health care company in the world.

I was definitely interested, but also concerned about how I could transfer to J&J without creating problems for myself and them. Regardless, I decided to pursue the opportunity. It so happened that my first conversation with them occurred on September 11, 2001.

I was in Washington, D.C., attending a PhRMA meeting and called my assigned J&J's HR person before the day's meeting began. We were talking when all of a sudden, he said, "Wow. My office windows face New York City and I see a lot of smoke coming from the World Trade Center towers." While concerned, we continued discussing the details of the job offer until we were alerted by colleagues that terrorists had attacked the twin towers and the Pentagon. Being in D.C., I experienced firsthand the extreme security measures that were taken to protect the capital city after it was discovered that a fourth hijacked airplane had been heading our direction before crashing in a field in Shanksville, Pennsylvania.

I was unable to travel for several weeks since all U.S. airspace was closed by the Federal Aviation Administration but otherwise, my work continued with few extra precautions. The one exception was the Friendship Bridge between Brazil and Paraguay in my Latin American territory. It was known that some al-Qaeda members traded on the Paraguayan side, so we had to be more careful there. Overall, however, the attacks did not affect our sales very much.

There were some people who believed we should ban our drugs in the Middle East when it was discovered that most of the terrorists on September 11 had come from Saudi Arabia. But when you're dealing with registered pharmaceuticals, boycotts and bans don't work. And morally, you can't stop providing lifesaving drugs to an entire region based on the actions of a handful of individuals. So we continued to sell the drugs to Saudi Arabia, Iraq, and throughout the Middle East.

While 9/11 largely left our business unaffected, the terrorist attacks had a profound impact on me personally. At that moment, more than any other, I realized how much the United States meant to me. I went through the naturalization process and obtained my citizenship status on January 3, 2003, at a ceremony in Cherry Hill, New Jersey. An American at last.

Several weeks after the attack, I finally got everything squared away with J&J's human-resources team and I met with Rick Lane to tell him I was leaving BMS for Johnson & Johnson. After unsuccessfully trying to persuade me to stay, he inquired whether I was going to work for Chris Poon. I honestly did not know at that point, but he seemed convinced that was the case and made it clear he would do whatever he could to impede the transfer.

He even went so far as to say that BMS would not allow me to work for J&J anywhere in New Jersey. I was shocked and angered that he would try to prevent me from earning my livelihood whichever way I wanted to do it. Chris Poon advised me to consult a good attorney about it, who assured me that no judge or jury would rule against me from earning a living in that state.

In October 2001, I joined J&J as company group chair managing Asia Pacific, Japan, and Latin America. I was one of approximately fifty people who eventually left BMS and moved over to J&J.

JOHNSON & JOHNSON

When I interviewed with William Weldon, chairman of the board of directors and CEO of J&J, three-quarters of our conversation revolved around the company credo: customers are first, followed by the community, employees, and stockholders, in that order. All Johnson & Johnson affiliates around the world followed the credo, which was crafted in 1943 by Robert Wood Johnson one year before the company went public. It's engraved in stone at the entrance of the company's headquarters in New Brunswick, New Jersey, and throughout my years with the company, I took it to heart.

My transition to J&J went smoothly. I felt welcome and reported directly to Chris Poon, with whom I had previously enjoyed a good working relationship.

Christine Poon and me, two friends at J&J.
New Brunswick, NJ, early 2000s.

As company group chair, I oversaw the pharmaceutical business in Asia Pacific, Japan, and Latin America. Our acronym was APJLA and my team became a close-knit group that primarily operated out of the New Brunswick office but frequently traveled together to our various affiliate operations.

My immediate focus was on Japan, China, India, Australia, Brazil, and Mexico. Even though I oversaw fifty countries in total, these six countries were the drivers of growth. It's not that we did not sell our product in all the other areas, too, but we didn't focus our attention as much on them because they just didn't have enough people to influence sales. As a public company, it was imperative to grow and show increased profitability so investors continued buying our stock. It was a fun challenge.

Another of my responsibilities was to establish the APJLA's annual budget and help develop the group's new strategic plan, which aimed to grow that arm of the business from $3 billion to $8 billion by 2020. Toward that effort, I focused on investing intelligently in the launch of new products and improving sales force effectiveness. At that time, we were spending more than $170 million in research and development, principally for trials in Japan, China, and India, which were overseen and administered by our outstanding research-and-development personnel. One new product for multiple myeloma gained a lot of attention and helped propel us toward our goal of double-digit growth of sales and profitability.

We also invested in our critical operations and worked with affinity groups within our New Brunswick office to promote a more diverse workforce, including Asians and Hispanics. Special attention was also paid to succession planning, which required every general manager to work closely with the HR department to find a qualified replacement before they left.

J&J Board of Directors and senior management. I am in the second row, the last person on the right. New Brunswick, NJ, early 2000s.

Xian-Janssen

Back in the 1950s, Johnson & Johnson was a consumer-product-only company. Then, in the early 1960s, they acquired Dr. Paul Janssen's pharmaceutical company in Belgium and licensed the products he had developed under the J&J brand. Dr. Janssen was not only a scientist, but also an illustrious gentleman and a well-rounded intellectual who was particularly interested in China. I met him a couple of times when he was in his late seventies/early eighties during my travels to Belgium for industry meetings.

In 1974, Dr. Janssen visited Xi'an, China—one of the ancient capitals of that country situated at the beginning of the Silk Road that extends all the way to Turkey—and its major archaeological site that contains the famed terracotta warriors. Fascinated by the city's history, he later persuaded J&J to establish its Chinese presence there when the country opened up to capitalism and foreign investment plans in the early 1980s.

Since that time, J&J had developed a well-respected, long-standing presence in Xi'an and built solid relationships with its officials, which allowed select J&J executives to visit the protected site of the terracotta warriors. When these statues were discovered and all the dirt that had protected them for three thousand years was removed, microorganisms attacked the soldiers, causing them to start to deteriorate. Fortunately, Dr. Janssen developed a treatment that saved these important artifacts.

Kathy and I stand among the terracotta warriors.
Xi'an, China, September 2002.

Back when Dr. Janssen set up the joint venture in Xi'an, he agreed to a 52/48 percent ownership. At that time, J&J was content with a small majority. However, I remembered the 90/10 partnership I had successfully established in a joint venture for Lilly. Recognizing the opportunity before me, I began to work toward a renegotiation. After all, we were providing all the innovation that was required and had continued to bring new products into the country over the years, even though that was not in the contract.

In addition, when the company first arrived in Xi'an in 1985, they built an apartment building to house their three hundred Chinese workers, many of whom would not have had a place to live otherwise. At that time, if the workers were fortunate enough to have a home at all, it was most likely a small mud house, particularly if they lived in the rural areas. So J&J provided them not only with a job, but also affordable housing. Housing continues to be a significant issue in China and other places in Asia like Singapore, where apartment dwellers must sign a ninety-nine-year lease or mortgage. Crazy.

The goal was not to bring in American employees but instead to develop a local Chinese workforce to run the operation. Of course, when they first set up the new manufacturing plant, they had to bring in a lot of expats who were specialists to start the process. But they also created a training center on-site where the expats were expected to train the locals so they could take over within three to four years; succession planning was important right from the beginning. J&J did this in each country—China, Brazil, Japan, Korea. The multinational expats played such an honorable role in developing these countries, which I think is beautiful. Sure, they signed on for the money, but they also left behind a huge legacy.

Over the years, these investments paid off and the company generated a lot of growth. By 2001, the company was selling millions of dollars, which led me to believe we deserved more of the profits. After explaining my reasoning, I successfully negotiated an ownership increase from 52 percent to 70 percent—an arrangement that more adequately reflected our contribution to the growth of the company.

Memorable Moments

As president of APJLA, I was a member of J&J's pharmaceutical group operating committee (GOC), which was led by Christine Poon. We met frequently to manage our global pharmaceutical efforts and once a year, we visited one of our affiliate countries to become more aware of their specific issues. Three visits in particular were extraordinarily impactful to me.

The first was our trip to Russia, which enabled us to meet the members of their local board. We invited the former president of the Soviet Union, Mikhail Gorbachev, to join us and we were pleased when he arrived in the midafternoon. He spoke with us for a few hours, answering a lot of questions about the politics of the moment, and we convinced him to stay for dinner. It was then that we had the opportunity to learn about his many meetings with President Reagan, a man whom he liked, but who ultimately disappointed him greatly.

After having achieved *perestroika* (economic freedom), Mr. Gorbachev was trying to achieve *glasnost* (political freedom) and reform communism, not eliminate it. But when President Reagan came to Berlin and said, "Mr. Gorbachev, tear down this wall," it created a momentum that was impossible to stop. "He should not have done that," Mr. Gorbachev said. Two years later, the wall did come down, uniting East and West Germany and effectively ending the Cold War.

Mikhail Gorbachev, former President of the Soviet Union (1990–1991), is seated in the front row, center, wearing a blue tie. I am standing directly behind him, wearing a red tie. J&J Pharmaceutical GOC meeting in Moscow, Russian Federation, mid-2000s.

The second impactful GOC trip was our visit to Brazil, where we met with the local cadre of managers and the country's former president, Fernando Henrique Cardoso. Mr. Cardoso spoke in English and captivated the entire group with his professional understanding of economics and politics. It was under his administration that Brazil adopted the new real currency in 1994 and protected patents for pharmaceuticals in 1996.

I was pleased to meet Fernando Henrique Cardoso (left), the President of Brazil from 1994 to 2002. J&J Pharmaceutical GOC meeting in São Paulo, S.P., Brazil, late 2000s.

The third was our initial GOC trip to Japan. Once the meeting arrangements had been made, our hosts asked us to send them the official headshot of each of the executives who would be in attendance. We submitted our photos and upon our arrival, they presented each of us with a handmade doll in our likeness. I actually received two dolls on that trip, and at a subsequent meeting, I received a third. One is dressed as business executive with a tie, another is more casually dressed, and the final one is dressed as a soccer player. It's an incredibly thoughtful cultural tradition.

Members of J&J Pharmaceutical GOC hold their personalized
handmade dolls. I'm in the front row, far right.
Tokyo, Japan, late 2000s.

While those were the three most impactful meetings for me, all of our meetings were valuable because they enabled the various members of the operating committee to connect with each other and their respective in-country team members. During the GOC trips, we also visited our various manufacturing plants and engaged with the local employees and regional managers, and on one occasion, we paid a visit to the former president of Brazil, José Sarney. Sarney was considered a friend of the industry and in his new position as president of the Brazilian Senate, he deserved our attention.

Members of the Latin American and Brazilian management team
visit with José Sarney, former President of the Senate of Brazil.
I'm standing in the center wearing the red tie; Sarney is standing
beside me (second from left). Brasília, D.F., Brazil, late 2000s.

Climbing Mt. Fuji

In late 2003, Chris Poon and I discussed how we had made many trips to Japan for business, yet we had never been able to explore the country. That was when we decided that we, along with our spouses and her two nephews, would climb Mt. Fuji, a dormant volcano near Tokyo. We set a date and asked our local affiliate to discover a guide (*sherpa*) and a translator for us, which we paid for.

We began our climb at three o'clock in the morning, each of us carrying a flashlight to illuminate our path as we joined several families with children and elderly Japanese individuals. The starting elevation was 2,000 meters and rose up to 3,776 meters (12,388 feet). The sunrise, clear skies, and glorious views were before us as we hiked up. Rest stops along the way helped, as did the sherpa's mantra, "Small steps, small steps." The last two hundred meters were steep; so steep that our translator refused to hike the final stretch. She sat down on a rock, opened her umbrella for shade, and awaited our return.

We reached the top by twelve o'clock; it had taken us nine hours. We stayed on the summit for about an hour, enjoying the panorama as we ate the sandwiches we had packed. Our descent took about six hours, and fog rolled in near the end, which made for some surreal moments. A loud rumbling noise turned out to belong to an orange earthmoving tractor. Later, we were startled when a man holding two horses suddenly emerged from the fog beside us.

The feeling of accomplishment as we neared the end was unlike any other I have ever experienced. We proudly learned to say, "I climbed Mt. Fuji" in Japanese before the euphoria turned into exhaustion. Even after resting overnight at a nearby inn, I discovered the next day that walking proved to be a challenge.

Our colleagues at the office in Tokyo were impressed by our feat. Amazingly, most of them had never tried to climb Mt. Fuji.

L-R: Christine Poon, her husband, Michael Tweedle, her nephews, Kathy, and me at the summit of Mt. Fuji, Japan, fall 2003.

Family Losses

Kathy and I were heartbroken when her father, Richard, passed away in 2007 and again, just one year later, when her mother, Rowena, passed in 2008. Richard had always been a strong supporter of my international commitments and Rowena frequently sent wonderful care packages from home. Both were our sounding boards when we house hunted, were wonderful companions on several of our vacations, and came to visit us at most of the places Kathy and I lived. They were also incredibly helpful, providing whatever we needed.

Once Kathy and I moved to New Jersey, we traveled frequently between Princeton and Pittsburgh to visit them. It was important to us, and we were thankful that we had been able to enjoy almost ten years of living closer to them before they passed.

On my side of the family, we lost Florisvaldo Joaquim, my sister Luzia's husband, in early 2008 due to diabetes complications. He had become my good friend and confidant when I lived in São Paulo between 1969 and 1974. Indeed, he had a calm influence on my entire family. Both he and Luzia were teachers in São Paulo for a number of years before he attended law school and became a lawyer. Then he joined the courts and served arrest warrants. He was a wonderful, intelligent gentleman.

Pharmaceutical Organizations

In addition to my job responsibilities, I represented J&J within PhRMA as chair of the Japan Steering Committee from 2003 to 2005 and chair of the international section from 2006 to 2009. Our efforts remained focused on intellectual property rights, pricing, and regulatory affairs.

From 2006 to 2008, I also served as a board member of the American Foundation for Pharmaceutical Education, whose mission is to advance and support pharmaceutical science education at U.S. schools and colleges of pharmacy, and from 2008 to 2010, I participated in the Council of the Americas, an organization founded and chaired by David Rockefeller to promote free markets and capitalism throughout the Americas. Every September, the Council of the Americas invited its member presidents and prime ministers to speak to us while they were in New York City attending the United Nations' General Assembly meetings. Luiz Inácio Lula da Silva, president of Brazil, and Michelle Bachelet, president of Chile, were two of the dignitaries who came to speak to us.

During one of the Council of the Americas meetings, I was seated next to David Rockefeller. I thought to myself, *Here I am, once this poor little kid from the boondocks of Brazil, now working alongside a member of the powerful Rockefeller family.* It was amazing to think about. I've always been a person to look at the glass as half-full; it's a great perspective to have. Everything is possible.

Growth Through Innovation

Throughout my career, I focused on growing companies and moving them into profitability through increased sales and productivity, which I accomplished by increasing volume, prices, or both. This required creativity and a willingness to take risks.

I often had to convince my boss to spend X amount more money because I believed we could deliver increased numbers. During my last year at J&J, for example, we were selling $3 billion but I believed we could sell $3.3 billion the next year.

"Whoa, you want to increase sales by $300 million?"

"Yes."

"Where are you going to make the increase?"

"By launching our new product, we can add $100 million in Japan, $50 million in Brazil, and $50 million in China. The remaining $100 million can be achieved by selling more of our existing products."

It was a huge risk to promise my boss that we'd increase sales by 10 percent to reach $3.3 billion in one year. I then had to work fast to create the infrastructure that would enable us to make good on my prediction. First, I hired and trained new sales reps. Then I had to work my tail off to motivate them. If you don't motivate them, they're not going to work as hard or sell as much. For example, we required them to call on ten doctors per day out of the two hundred physicians on their roster. But if we had motivated sellers, they would want to do more than that, maybe visit twelve or thirteen instead of just ten.

I believe that every sales force—with perhaps the exception of a unionized sales force—can immediately start selling more if they want to. My job was to motivate and creatively enable them to sell more within the countries with the largest population. If we couldn't make it in those six or so countries, we wouldn't reach the goal. So I regularly flew to those countries to motivate the sales teams and keep them accountable to reach their objectives.[41]

Global Initiatives

During my nine years with J&J, I was involved in two major initiatives that were transformational for millions of people.

The first initiative took place in April 2002 when J&J acquired Tibotec, a company founded by Dr. Paul Stoffels, who eventually became head of research at J&J. They were in the process of developing anti-retrovirals for the treatment of AIDS. At the time, it was estimated that forty million people were suffering from the disease worldwide.

Once the drugs cleared the clinical trials and became available, J&J put me in charge of launching them in Russia, China, Thailand, South Africa, India, Brazil, and Mexico—the countries with the most HIV infection at that time. The new products significantly reduced the viral load to the point that HIV became undetectable. When an infected person received the drugs, they could live with HIV, no problem. Before that, an HIV diagnosis was a death sentence.

In order to provide these HIV products to as many people as possible in the developing world, we decided to make them low cost. We reduced the normal charge of $30 per day of therapy, which was what people were paying in the U.S., to just $2 per day of therapy. J&J called it the Market Access Initiative. I called it "doing well by doing good."

The second major initiative was J&J's decision in 2006/2007 to become a sponsor of the 2008 Beijing Olympics. Given our significant

---

[41] Since I retired from the company in March 2010, I was not able to personally see the $3.3 billion come to reality, but I was satisfied in knowing that I helped set the stage for their success.

presence in China, the company committed to earmark significant funds for the project, and the Xian-Janssen division was tasked with how to best represent the company as a major Olympic sponsor.

My team from the U.S. supported their efforts and together, we helped build our presence at the Games in a significant way. I was able to attend the grand opening and felt that the millions of people attending the event live and watching on TV received an improved understanding of how J&J's pharmaceuticals, medical devices, and consumer products could benefit them.

New Horizons

In 2009, Christine Poon retired from her position as global chairperson of pharmaceuticals at J&J to become the new dean of the Fisher College of Business at Ohio State University. Over the years, she and I had often spoken about academia and its importance in the development of young men and women. At one point, she suggested that an administrative role in academia could be a good position for me as well, given my PhD, previous academic teaching experience, and thirty years in business.

Thus, as I began my own retirement preparations in March 2010, I began to investigate academic opportunities. After interviewing with several universities, I received an offer to become the business school dean for West Virginia University. The president of WVU, Jim Clements, wanted to hire a nontraditional dean and I fit the bill.

After growing J&J's APJLA arm to over $3 billion in sales in more than fifty countries, managing more than nine thousand employees, and operating six different manufacturing plants around the world, I was ready to enter academia.

IMAGINATION AT ITS BEST

When the anti-retrovirals developed by Tibotec were nearing the launch stage, we tapped Wlodeck Kubiak, one of our brilliant executives in Poland, as the lead for the Market Access Initiative, who reported to me. Our initiative had to do many things, but two things were at the top of the list.

First, we had to establish relationships with critical NGOs such as Médecins Sans Frontières, Oxfam, Bill & Melinda Gates Foundation, Clinton Foundation, and PEPFAR (the U.S. State Department organization that was at the forefront of providing financial support to the developing world). PEPFAR was one of President George W. Bush's most significant initiatives in the area of international public health, which has appropriated more than $90 billion since its inception.

Second, we had to meet people on the ground in the developing countries most affected by AIDS, which were Russia, China, Thailand, India, South Africa, Brazil, and Mexico. I personally visited China, Brazil, and Mexico, but Wlodeck visited them all.

We discovered that some of these countries, such as Brazil, already had intelligent systems in place to deliver the drugs and they had the ability to buy the drugs themselves. Others, like South Africa, were still discussing whether AIDS was due to HIV infection and therefore had no systems in place. We worked with each of the governments to help them receive and distribute the low-cost lifesaving drugs, and we relied on PEPFAR to help us eliminate the associated import taxes. All these efforts positively shaped the external environment.

For each of us at J&J, the Market Access Initiative was earth-shattering and served as an example of how to "do well by doing good."

The Big Picture

2000s Overview

WORLD / U.S. [42]

- Dow:[43] 11,497.12–10,428.05, –9.3%
- 9/11 dominates the decade and gives rise to two wars: Operation Iraqi Freedom (Iraq, 2003–2011) and Operation Enduring Freedom (Afghanistan, 2001–2021)
- International Criminal Court convenes in 2002
- *Harry Potter* best-selling books and movies are released
- Indonesian tsunami kills 230,000 in 2004
- Social networks start: Twitter, Facebook, etc.
- Hurricane Katrina overwhelms New Orleans in 2005
- New wars: Niger Delta, Houthi insurgency, Mexican drug war
- Climate change grows in importance
- Great Recession begins with housing/credit crisis in the U.S. in 2008
- Internet drives globalization
- Euro notes and coins enter circulation in 2002
- Saddam Hussein is executed in 2006
- Video game consoles grow in popularity

---

42 Source of historical data in this section: "2000s," Wikimedia Foundation, https://en.wikipedia.org/wiki/2000s. Last accessed September 26, 2023.

43 Source of the Dow range in this section: "Dow Jones Industrial Average," Wikimedia Foundation, https://en.wikipedia.org/wiki/Dow_Jones_Industrial_Average. Last accessed October 24, 2023.

BRAZIL

- Fernando Henrique Cardoso, Luiz Inácio Lula da Silva
- Growth is driven by commodities (higher prices and volume from China)
- Brazil wins soccer World Cup in Japan in 2002
- The economy reaches $1.57 billion; remains #8 in the world

PERSONAL SIGNIFICANT EVENTS / ACHIEVEMENTS

- Lives in Hopewell/Princeton, New Jersey
- BMS, Princeton (2000–2001)
- President, Latin America, Puerto Rico, Canada
- Chair, Canada Steering Committee, PhRMA (2000–2001)
- Chair, Latin-America Steering Committee, PhRMA (2001–2003)
- J&J, New Brunswick, New Jersey (2001–2010)
- Company Group Chair, Asia Pacific, Japan, Latin America (APJLA)
- Chair, Japan Steering Committee, PhRMA (2003–2005)
- Chair, International Section Steering Committee, PhRMA (2006–2009)
- Board member, Council of the Americas (2008–2010)
- Board member, American Foundation for Pharmaceutical Education (2006–2008)

LOSSES

- Richard Strong, January 5, 2007
- Florisvaldo Joaquim, January 4, 2008
- Rowena Strong, May 11, 2008

7

THE ACADEMY AT LAST

WEST VIRGINIA UNIVERSITY (WVU), MILAN PUSKAR DEAN, COLLEGE OF BUSINESS AND ECONOMICS (2010–2015)

Transitioning as a top-level executive with a Fortune 100 company to dean of a business school required me—and those hiring me—to give flight to imagination. Typically, academia is a traditional, tight-knit hierarchy—you work your way up from a professor to a chair to a provost and then to a dean. I was fortunate that West Virginia University's president, Jim Clements, didn't want to hire a professor who had been teaching the same syllabus for thirty-five years. He wanted someone from big business who was invigorated by competition and international opportunities. Since I met those qualifications, I got the job in the summer of 2010.

A few weeks before I assumed my new position in West Virginia, I was in Lima, Peru, attending my last official J&J meeting when I received a call from Evandro, my nephew in Brazil. "Dear Uncle, I have some news to share—my father passed away today." Carlito, my second brother, the singer and composer, had killed himself after a long struggle with depression and alcoholism. Kathy and I flew to São Paulo to attend the funeral the next day. This shook the whole family, and we are still trying to process it today.

The deanship I assumed was named after Milan Puskar, a first-generation Serbian American who founded Mylan Pharmaceuticals in Morgantown, the home of WVU. He grew his company to two thousand employees before eventually selling it to Pfizer. I was honored to meet him before his death in 2011, and I was grateful for how supportive both he and his daughter were of WVU. In fact, he had such high regard for the university that he made sure his tombstone in town faced the campus.

I soon learned that West Virginia University is highly regarded throughout the entire state. While on a bus tour with other new hires as part of our orientation, I was delighted to discover that the blue-and-gold bus was greeted enthusiastically along the way and that Mountaineer flags were displayed in the front yards of many homes.

Kathy and I were warmly welcomed into the Morgantown community and moved into a house overlooking Cheat Lake. Like most neighborhoods there, ours had once been the site of a coal mine, but you would never know it by looking at the beautifully restored landscape.

Left: West Virginia University, Evansdale Campus, Morgantown, WV, early 2010s.
Right: West Virginia University, Downtown Campus, Morgantown, WV, early 2010s.

WVU students and the community pack Milan Puskar Stadium to
support our Mountaineer football team,
Morgantown, WV, early 2010s.

I was excited to give my first speech as Milan Puskar
Dean of WVU College of Business and Economics,
Morgantown, WV, May 4, 2010.

I'm surrounded by my staff in the office of the dean, B&E,
Morgantown, WV, mid-2010s.

Our third home, Morgantown, WV, 2010.

BETTER, BIGGER, RANKED

The College of Business and Economics (B&E) at WVU in early 2010 was an institution comprised of more than 2,000 students from thirty-six states and forty-two countries, close to 150 faculty and staff, and a budget of more than $30 million. The college also had more than 20,000 alumni around the world, many of whom proved to be important allies in our mission to fund school improvements.

Upon my arrival, I worked with faculty and staff to create a new vision for the college: Better, Bigger, Ranked. We then developed five strategic priorities that guided us as we aimed to transform B&E from a good to a vibrant college.

I soon appeared on the front cover of *b&e Magazine*, West Virginia University, spring 2011.

Strategic Priority 1 - Attract / Retain

Our top priority was to increase enrollment, which required paying attention to details and developing a more well-rounded program to attract new students to WVU instead of our competitors. After much research and brainstorming, we changed the college to a four-year institution with a focus on internships and moved to direct admissions to help students transition from high school straight into a college career path.

Previously, students took two years of general studies before they chose a particular career path. With direct admissions, incoming students entered the career schools of their choice from the moment they were accepted. Since this required a heavier course load and concentrated study than most high school graduates were accustomed to, I established a mentoring center to help them succeed.

We also established an online Executive MBA program, enrolling more than two hundred students from twenty-one states and Canada with an average of 10.3 years of working experience. The *U.S. News and World Report* ranked our program the twenty-third best online program in the country, six positions better than the previous year. We launched a PhD in business administration to complement our forty-eight-year-old PhD in economics and strengthened global recruiting, particularly in China, Brazil, and Germany. By the fall of 2013, all these initiatives enabled us to set an all-time enrollment record of 2,597 students.

Strategic Priority 2 - Educate / Advance Research

Raising our rank was one of the first things I focused on with the MBA. Our average Graduate Management Aptitude Test score had been about 535, but over three years, we increased it to 620. And in

2014, *U.S. News and World Report* listed our MBA program in the top one hundred of the country.

Another pivotal change was our new partnerships with WVU's fifteen "sister" colleges to launch new joint MBA programs in the fields of medicine, pharmacy, dentistry, public health, and engineering. We already offered MBAs for law and sports management, but I believed it was important to offer these additional MBA programs to not only attract new students, but also retain many of the existing undergraduate students for a couple extra years.

Of the new MBAs, the two most popular were pharmacy and nursing. Lots of students used them to grow their careers. The medical MBA, however, wasn't as successful. We quickly discovered that doctors who have already gone through med school and are working aren't as motivated to go back to school to earn an MBA. As for premed students, it's hard to put off a residency program to do an MBA—it doesn't make any sense. But the other programs worked well.

Additional areas of focus included new undergraduate programs, hiring research-focused faculty, and strengthening the teaching of business ethics, which led to WVU receiving a #5 ranking for undergraduate business schools for ethics by *Bloomberg Businessweek*.

We also launched a new B&E Distinguished Speaker Series with successful leaders from academia, business, and government sharing their life stories, career insights, and leadership lessons. These speakers, still at the peak of their careers, served as role models and proved to be both informational and motivational as the students prepared to get their start in the world.

Strategic Priority 3 - Enable / Place

The Center for Career Development worked to attract more employers to campus for job interviews and also prepared undergraduates for the job market. Students were firmly encouraged to apply for internships to gain experience, which increased by 63 percent. By the time I left, more than two hundred companies regularly recruited on campus, including sixty Fortune 500 companies.

Strategic Priority 4 - Organize / Engage

The college significantly engaged with the local business community, state government, and general public. We regularly held Economic Outlook Conferences throughout the state to encourage better decision making among government and business officials, and information from these conferences was shared by our professors at a joint session of the WV House of Delegates and Senate every January. The College of Business and Economics also created the monthly "Mountain State Business Index" that was published by the *West Virginia State Journal*.

Engaging with the community meant I participated in live interviews with the state media and was a regular on the "Decision Makers" show, a program of news, variety, and analysis run by Bray Cary, a WVU graduate.

We continued the Roll of Distinguished Alumni of the College of Business and Economics that recognized and honored alumni achievements. We also created the West Virginia Hall of Fame program to recognize men and women in industry, government, and academia whose work had impacted West Virginia, the nation, and the world. At the first ceremony, West Virginia Governor Earl Ray Tomblin introduced the event and recognized the impact I was already making on WVU.

Corporate social responsibility was emphasized at B&E, allowing students to learn through hands-on philanthropy. More than 250 students have taken the class and given out more than $250,000 to hundreds of needy institutions in Morgantown and throughout north-central West Virginia.

But perhaps the most significant component of organizing and engaging was the creation of four new academic centers to help students succeed at WVU. The Center for Entrepreneurship supported innovative thinkers, the Robbins Center for Global Business and Strategy expanded our global footprint, and the Center for Free Enterprise expanded research and taught the principles of how a free society influences the wealth of nations. The fourth center, the Confucius Institute, was formed in partnership with the Tianjin University of Finance and Economics in China to strengthen cultural and educational ties between the U.S. and China.

We weren't the only university to create a Confucious center; the Chinese government has initiated more than one hundred such institutes on college campuses across America. The Confucius Institutes have now become somewhat controversial because they may want to change their contracts. Back in 2013/2014, the contract we signed with them clearly stated that all hiring decisions were the sole responsibility of the university; the Chinese would not participate in that aspect of it at all. But soon they started to say, "We have three Chinese who just arrived in the U.S. We'd like them to be professors at the Confucian Center." We had to repeatedly tell them to stop trying to bring in their own people. We were very welcoming of the money, and we were willing to teach about China—even about Confucianism—but I was adamant that the university was going to remain independent to its core.

Over time, all our efforts toward greater global engagement started to pay off and the number of international students at B&E went from 73 in 2010 to 198 in 2013. Partnerships with key universities were sought and signed in the belief that studying abroad leads to increased understanding and knowledge between countries.

I was happy to meet WV Governor, Earl Ray Tomblin, 2011.

This photo from the campus magazine shows me giving a motivational speech to B&E students, early 2010s.

Strategic Priority 5 - Fund / Build

The aforementioned initiatives, combined with effective fundraising efforts and judicious management of resources (aided by a terrific economist I hired in 2012 who ended up later becoming dean of B&E), enabled us to become a financially sound college.

Our fundraising alone reached an all-time record of $34 million (2.5 times the amount raised in the previous campaign), which allowed us to construct new centers; fund scholarships; add more professorships, fellowships, and assistantships; and create great programs.

I was heavily involved in the fundraising efforts, identifying potential donors and traveling around the country to meet with them. I personally secured $3 million from one donor to create the center for entrepreneurship and initiated the request for $10 million from another donor to construct the new College of Business and Economics.[44] On August 26, 2022, I attended the inauguration of the new B&E building. It was wonderful to be welcomed back by everyone and to see the great state of West Virginia again.

Announcement of $3 million donation from BrickStreet Insurance.
L–R: Jim Clements, WVU President; Gregory Burton, President and CEO of BrickStreet Mutual Insurance Company; me; and Oliver Luck, Athletic Director of WVU.

ONE GLOBAL WVU

Jim Clements was highly regarded for his leadership, openness, and sincere concern for the students. A few months before his departure to become Clemson's next president in 2013, he created a new position

---

44 On November 9, 2018, the B&E college was renamed the John Chambers College of Business and Economics after the two-time WVU alumnus.

just for me: chief global officer over all WVU. I would serve in this capacity alongside my dean position at B&E.

At that time, WVU had more than thirty-two thousand students from across the U.S. and from more than 110 countries. This was good, but it could be better. Since one of the key areas that needed to be addressed was our limited international partnerships, I put together the One Global WVU Engagement Task Force. Our vision was to expand our global footprint and deepen our global engagement. One Global WVU was overseen by the Office of International Students and Scholars and the Office of International Programs, who reviewed, changed, and enforced new processes within our study-abroad exchange programs.

We needed more international students to participate in the program—our goal was to have three thousand international students come to WVU to study—but first, we had to put adequate infrastructure in place. Therefore, we proactively created a plan to provide housing, transportation, community support, and student-placement jobs after they graduated.

We then began to ramp up our marketing efforts, reaching out to qualified study-abroad sponsor organizations such as Fulbright, the Institute of International Education, and international universities. We promoted the advantages of studying at a large university like West Virginia, which offered targeted curriculum, great faculty, beautiful campuses, and enjoyable events.

By strategically recruiting from fourteen high-potential country markets, participating in key international fairs, and utilizing our existing seven alumni chapters overseas, we significantly increased our international student, scholar, and professional applications.

In addition, we developed 3+1 programs and similar modalities with international universities. These programs allowed students to study three years in their own country, then come to us to complete the final year of their degree, thereby earning two degrees (a U.S. degree and a degree from their home country).

I traveled to China to attend the opening of the official Shanghai chapter of the WVU Alumni Association, Shanghai, China, November 10, 2013.

All these things combined were transformational. It is just amazing how much of the plan was achieved. With the vision and the strategic plan's five priorities, we were able to grow the college into a vibrant and competitive institution.

The faculty and staff at the college played a significant role in our success as well. Staff members worked or ran programs for students and parents on weekends. They traveled to lead sessions for MBA programs out of state and manned booths at the WV State Fair each year. Faculty members made sure to attend graduation ceremonies, where they took the time to greet the students and their parents afterwards with genuine sincerity. It was an honor to work with such dedicated staff.

At the end of each school year, I looked forward to leading the commencement ceremonies for the business school graduates. It was wonderful to greet parents and grandparents, listen to esteemed speakers share their wisdom with the class, and hear the student speakers address their peers. Each ceremony was a heartwarming reminder of how the long years of hard work culminated at that moment as the tassels on the mortarboards were moved from right to left.

Leading the Way to a New Opportunity

Understanding the value of business relationships, I selectively joined organizations that allowed us to put WVU and B&E on the map. I became a member of Bio West Virginia and the West Virginia Chamber of Commerce Education Task Force and served on the board and executive committee of the Blanchette Rockefeller Neurosciences Institute at WVU. I also served on the board of Emcure Pharmaceuticals, an Indian generic pharmaceutical company, and I especially valued my time on the board and finance committee of the WV United Health System.

As a natural leader who is generally extroverted and engaging and as someone who always wants to be active, I enjoyed the opportunities to partner with people, try new things, and push our initiatives forward. I heard from certain alumni and friends of the college that more was done at B&E during my five years there than what other institutions had accomplished in twenty. But I couldn't have done it alone. The amount of support the college received from the administration, faculty, students, alumni, and the community was a driving factor to the school's growth and the strategic plan's success.

Based on my track record as dean of B&E, many people wanted me to become president of West Virginia University after Jim Clements left. Indeed, I had hoped to do just that, but the Board of Governors offered the position to Gordon Gee, who accepted the position for the second time. The town was quite fond of Gordon from his earlier stint as president before he left for Ohio State.

Meeting the new boss of WVU, Gordon Gee. WVU, B&E, early 2014.

Disappointed but determined, I applied for various presidency positions across the country. I interviewed at several universities, but the one institution that stood out was the University of North Carolina Wilmington (UNCW).

When I interviewed with them in 2015, it seemed that both the search committee and the president of the UNC system were interested in bringing a nontraditional chancellor to campus. Eventually, I was approved by the Board of Governors and my future suddenly became intertwined with the words teal, marine science, longleaf pine, southeastern North Carolina, and Go Seahawks!

UNIVERSITY OF NORTH CAROLINA WILMINGTON (UNCW), CHANCELLOR, 2015–2022

The opportunity to become a University of North Carolina chancellor was one of the best experiences I ever had. I was told by the search committee that they wanted someone who was out of the ordinary; not your typical run-of-the-mill professor, but someone with the skills to manage a growing organization. UNCW was a mid-size university with 15,000 students, but I had run big corporations and was confident I could handle the job. In fact, I considered it a personal challenge to successfully do something out of the ordinary. By the time I left the university, it had grown to 18,030 students.

Perhaps the only drawback to the position was the limited ability to travel. A chancellor spends 90 percent of his or her time on the campus. You may travel within your state to attend important meetings, and you may occasionally travel across the country to woo potential donors, but you're basically tethered to one location.

I joined UNCW on July 1, 2015, and I was officially inaugurated nine months later. It was a wonderful ceremony attended by students, staff, faculty, trustees, friends like Christine Poon, and family members. Members of Kathy's family attended, as well as my youngest sister Luzia, who flew in from Brazil with my best friends, Sergio Laureano and his wife, Maria.

The ceremony was held on the oak-lined lawn in front of the original three buildings that comprised the campus in 1947 when it was known as Wilmington College. My speech reflected my vision for UNCW's future, Christine spoke about my career, and I swore an oath to the state of North Carolina on a Bible held by Kathy.

UNCW main campus, Wilmington, NC, mid-2010s.

Star-News article, "The Future of UNCW," April 23, 2015.

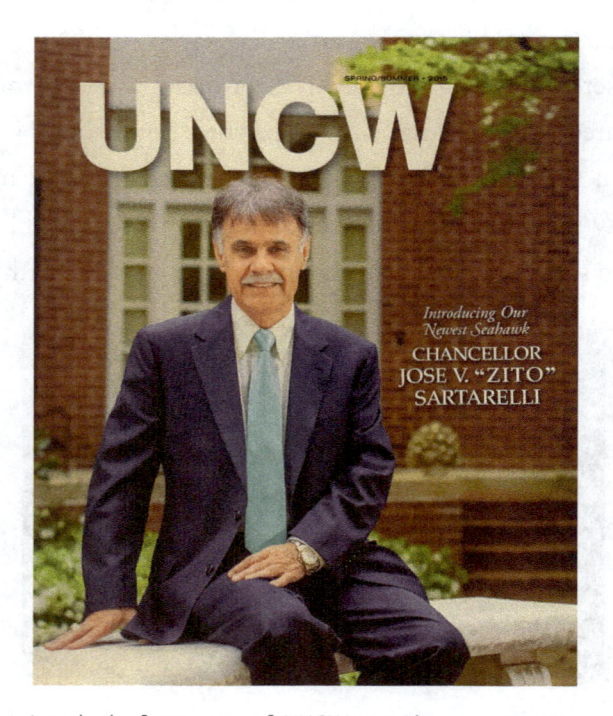

I made the front cover of *UNCW* magazine, summer 2015.

Chancellors together at my installation, UNCW, March 31, 2016. L-R: Dr. William A. Sederburg (UNCW Interim Chancellor), me, Dr. Rosemary DePaolo (UNCW Chancellor from 2003 to 2011), and Dr. James Leutze (UNCW Chancellor from 1990 to 2003).

Working Together

I reported directly to the president of the UNC system and worked under four different presidents during my seven-year tenure—Tom Ross (a judge and former president of Davidson College), Margaret Spellings (former U.S. secretary of education under President George W. Bush), William Roper (former president of UNC Health), and Peter Hans (former president of the Community College System of North Carolina). Each of them provided me with excellent support and represented the university well with the UNC Board of Governors, the controlling body of the UNC system.

I also worked closely with UNCW's local Board of Trustees, who were my partners in developing and overseeing the strategic plan for the university. Each member of the board was nominated by the NC Senate and the House since the legislature ultimately determines how the designated money (currently $3.2 billion a year) will be distributed within the statewide education system.

I am seated, third from right, with the UNCW Board of Trustees chaired by Michael Shivar (seated, far right), 2015–2016.

I am seated, fourth from right, with the UNC-system Board of Governors during their visit to the UNCW campus, March 2018.

Because the UNC system has such deep roots in the state's political system, I relied on UNCW's government affairs vice-chancellor, Mark Lanier, to facilitate my understanding of critical policies and procedures. He knew exactly when and what would happen concerning approvals, votes, and speeches related to the UNC system and effectively lobbied for the desired results. I was also assisted by many other competent staff (referred to as my cabinet) that advised me on all aspects of the campus.

My cabinet and I worked closely with the Faculty Senate and its steering committee, the Staff Senate and its president, and the Board of the Student Government Association, meeting at least once monthly with the presidents of these three organizations.

In addition, we were in constant contact with the Alumni Association, Friends of UNCW, the Board of Visitors, the Foundation Board, and the Endowment Board. Regular meetings with them allowed us to hear their viewpoints and discuss issues. Gatherings during the holiday season at the Kenan House, where Kathy and I resided, were wonderful opportunities to build their enthusiasm and loyalty to UNCW.

Extensive communication, both internal and external, was critical in my position. I worked closely with the Office of University Relations and its chief communications officer to conduct frequent PR interviews with local radio and television stations. In addition, videos were filmed to commemorate special events, such as the seventy-year anniversary of Wilmington College/UNCW in 2017 and the placement of the Seahawk Nest statue crafted by artist Dumay Gorham in 2021.

The Strategic Plan

The first project I faced upon my arrival was the development of a new five-year strategic plan. Working with the Board of Trustees, I organized a committee that spent approximately a year conducting research and creating the framework of the plan. When complete, it consisted of the following vision, mission, critical values, and strategic priorities:

Vision: UNCW will be recognized for its all-encompassing excellence, its global mindset, and its community engagement.

Mission: UNCW, the state's coastal university, is dedicated to the integration of teaching and mentoring with research and service. Our commitment to student engagement, creative inquiry, critical thinking, thoughtful expression, and responsible citizenship is expressed in our baccalaureate and master programs, as well as doctoral programs in areas of expertise that serve our state's needs. Our culture reflects our values of diversity and globalization, ethics and integrity, and excellence and innovation.

Critical Values: Excellence, Diversity, Integrity, Innovation, Student-Centered Focus, and Community Engagement.

Strategic Priorities: Attract/Retain, Educate/Advance Research, Enable/Place, Organize/Engage, and Fund/Build.

To prevent the plan from being put on a shelf and never being seen again, we decided that every October, I would update the Board of Trustees on how the plan was coming along. At each meeting, I shared the most recent metrics for each of the five strategic priorities, which enabled us to gauge whether we were on track to meet our goals.

Although the priorities were the same as those during my time at WVU, the goals attached to each priority were unique to UNCW and included customized metrics and timing. Over the next five years, we diligently pursued these priorities, which often required us to think outside the box and try new things.

Left: *Star-News* article, "A New and Bold Vision for UNCW,"
August 30, 2015.
Right: Another *Star-News* write-up about my work as Chancellor
of UNCW, March 31, 2016.

Attract / Retain

As we considered how to attract and retain more students, I realized the university had never fully tapped into the state's community college system. Excited about the potential, I personally contacted every one of the colleges, either by phone or in person. No other chancellor had ever done that. Why not? Perhaps because they didn't think the community college system was important. But the way I looked at it, these fifty-eight colleges throughout North Carolina were comprised of more than seven hundred thousand students. What an opportunity! This was a great place to "go fishing" for students.

Another source to boost enrollment was the military. We focused most of our attention on Camp Lejeune since they're nearby and we already enjoyed a strong partnership with them, but we also gained some students from Fort Liberty. UNCW now has more than two thousand military-connected students—those who are either active-duty service members, family members (children or spouses of service members), or veterans. To honor their presence on campus, we decided to rename our allied health building as Veterans Hall. We are the only university in the country to do so. The building features a substantial military lounge on the first floor, along with a small USO office that is staffed by a military person.

Brigadier General Niebel (fifth from the left), Commandant of Camp Lejeune, visits UNCW in 2021. Photo credit: Jeff Janowski.

Additional ways I helped recruit students was by attending education fairs and taking advantage of the fact that southeastern North Carolina has become one of the top relocation destinations in the country. Only Florida and Texas outpace us in this regard.

One of the downsides to this growth, however, is that it can attract more competition. For example, Northeastern University—the private research university in Boston—now has a branch campus offering an MBA program in Charlotte. Large universities like that are crossing state lines big time. That's one of the reasons I wanted to establish an engineering program at UNCW; I did not want to allow a different engineering school to crop up in Wilmington. It's always good to stay one step ahead of the competition.

Some of the key results of our efforts were that we brought in over three thousand students in seven years, enabling UNCW to become the fastest-growing university in the UNC system. We were also attracting quality students (our number of honor students grew significantly between 2015–2022), and our nursing school became the largest in North Carolina.

UNCW freshman class, fall 2017.

Educate / Advance Research

During my tenure, we drove growth through twenty new educational programs that included coastal engineering, system engineering, data science, masters in nursing, and four new PhDs. These were degrees that students wanted and enabled us to stand out from among our competitors. For example, we added an executive MBA program that a lot of doctors from Duke take online; we usually have at least five or six doctors in every session. It may take them two to five years to complete the program, but they love it. They told me, "Chapel Hill wants $125,000 for their MBA and you have to attend in person. But

UNCW allows me to do it on my time, at my own pace. And you charge me $25,000. Perfect."

Such programs enabled us to grow our revenues through volume, not price, since UNCW had government-mandated fixed-price tuition we could not change. Our tuition and fees only cost about $7,000—one of the lowest prices for a public university in any state of the country.

Research was also a key component to the strategic plan. We advanced differentiated research efforts from drug discovery and development to biometrics and space-based marine science. UNCW was one of the first universities in the country to send a nano-satellite into space; in fact, *Seahawk 1* continues to track the oceans on a regular basis.

Enable / Place

Quality partnerships are critical to the success of any organization. In the case of UNCW, we needed to develop relationships that would enable our students to reach their full potential. Toward that effort, we grew our corporate partnerships within the U.S. to include 228 different Fortune 500 companies. Close connections with some of Wilmington's largest businesses and institutions such as the New Hanover Regional Medical Center, New Hanover County Schools, General Electric, Corning, Live Oak Bank, and Quality Chemicals allowed UNCW students to advance careers through internships, employment, and socioeconomic mobility. In addition, through deep engagement with the region's business community, we experienced a record number of start-ups.

Because today's business world is global in nature, offering international opportunities was also critical. Therefore, we focused on sending our students to universities around the world and attracting foreign students to UNCW. Our International Programs Office led these efforts and I personally initiated partnerships with the University of Gibraltar and several in Brazil, including Insper—a private university in São Paulo—and some of the country's federal public universities, one of which is very close to my hometown.

During my tenure, UNCW partnered with a total of 119 international universities, which resulted in UNCW ranking fifth among its peers nationally for study-abroad programs in the 2018/2019 school year. When Kathy and I traveled abroad on holiday or for official university business, we often visited some of these partners. Our visit to Maynooth University outside Dublin, Ireland, was particularly memorable.

Our goal was to send 1,500 of our students to study overseas; we reached 1,000 students before the pandemic hit. We're just now starting to return to that original level. As for receiving international students to our campus, we grew from approximately 250 to about 700. It cannot be overstated how many local individuals and groups welcomed these foreign students throughout their stay here. Eventually, we'd like to receive 2,000–3,000 international students.

One thing that I think will help us get there is the 3+1+1 program we launched with the Chongqing University of Arts and Science in the Sichuan province of China. Sichuan is a prosperous region that contains approximately 200 million people—more than half of the U.S. population in just this one province. Through our partnership, their students study mathematics and English in China for three years and then they come to us for the fourth year. Following the successful completion of the program, they receive two diplomas: one from Chongqing and one from UNCW for their bachelor degree in mathematics. Thirty-three students enrolled in the pilot program in 2020 and nine of them arrived at UNCW in the fall of 2023. They can stay for their masters, too, if they wish. It's a great program of exchange that will undoubtedly allow us to bring in more students.

Dr. Aswani K. Volety, the current chancellor of UNCW, is also interested in increasing the international student population, particularly from his home country of India. The challenge, however, is personal finances. In China, students are capable of paying for their tuition and studying abroad, but that's a challenge for many Indian students. Scholarships may need to be developed.

Organize / Engage

Engaging with the community was a priority for us. We continued to facilitate the Isaac Bear Early College High School in conjunction with the New Hanover County superintendent of schools. This high school, which was built in 2006 on the campus of UNCW, has turned into one of the best not only in the city, but also the entire southeastern region. Many of its students go on to attend some of the best universities in the state and the country, including UNCW.

In addition, after many discussions with leading members of the general assembly, I was encouraged to pick a low-performing county school and improve its student outcomes. The Board of Trustees and I looked carefully at the options in New Hanover County and in 2018, we selected D.C. Virgo, a middle school that had received an F in their last evaluation. Its principal works in conjunction with the dean of UNCW's Watson School of Education and the school is overseen by a highly qualified board, of which I was a member. Progress has been made, but much more remains to be done to attain a higher score.

Fund / Build

One of the most critical components of any strategic plan is funding. Without it, little else in the plan can be accomplished. Therefore, we immediately began discussing a new $100 million capital campaign. There was much debate and brainstorming over what to name it, but ultimately we agreed on "Like No Other." UNCW is, in many respects, very different from the other universities in the UNC system. One of the biggest differentiators is our campus location—only four miles away from the ocean, we offer the only marine science program on the water in North Carolina.

UNCW Center for Marine Science, Wilmington, NC, mid-2010s.

We launched the initial silent phase of the campaign in the fall of 2016, during which time those of us on the committee personally reached out to companies, organizations, and alumni throughout the country to secure approximately 80 percent of the goal. Once that milestone was reached, we entered the public phase to garner the remaining 20 percent.

My fundraising efforts primarily took place in North Carolina, New Mexico, and Texas. One of our largest donors is a married couple who retired to Santa Fe, New Mexico, so I visited them there to ensure their continued support. I traveled to Dallas and Austin, Texas, to secure financial gifts from many of UNCW's highly successful and influential alumni who live there. And, of course, I drove throughout North Carolina to meet with both individuals and companies. Three of the university's largest corporate donors were, not surprisingly, local to Wilmington: New Hanover Regional Medical Center, General Electric, and Corning.

I present Yousry and Linda Sayed a Seahawk statue in commemoration of their $5 million gift to UNCW in 2018.

Rob Burrus (right) and I (left) shake hands with David Congdon (center) who gave a $10 million gift to UNCW to create the Congdon School of Supply Chain, Business Analytics, and Information Systems, 2018. Photo credit: Jeff Janowski.

Now that the county-owned New Hanover Regional Medical Center has been acquired by the corporate-owned Novant Health, the hospital's president no longer lives in the community. Dr. Volety can't just pick up the phone and invite him or her out for coffee to strengthen the relationship anymore. But one benefit of the hospital now being part of a large corporation is that they have a foundation. Since foundations are required to annually disburse 5 percent of their funds to retain their nonprofit status, Novant's foundation of $1.2 billion has to give out approximately $50–$60 million every year. UNCW will want to be one of their beneficiaries.

At the conclusion of the "Like No Other" campaign, we were all elated by the progress made. We achieved a record revenue of $458 million in 2020–2021 and a total investment of $770 million over seven years; that's three-quarters of a billion dollars. We received more money than anybody in the system, by far, and no company has ever invested $770 million in Wilmington or the southeastern region of the state, for that matter. It was a huge accomplishment.

We used $66 million of it to construct the new allied health building, which we renamed Veterans Hall. We also decided to remodel and expand the library, which was built in 1987, back when we only had about five thousand students. Now the library needs to accommodate its existing eighteen thousand students as well as thousands more future students. Thus, we're expanding the library by forty thousand square feet and remodeling the existing building at the cost of $62 million. It's expected to open in 2024.

We completed twenty-three construction projects total. These included a new dining hall, three new parking lots, a new film studio, an indoor batting cage for baseball, and an $8 million Center for Marine Sciences building (which would also house the new coastal engineering program). We also built a new softball field thanks to a $5 million donation, and Starbucks paid to construct a coffee shop in the middle of campus.

Veterans Hall on the campus of UNCW, mid-2010s.
Photo credit: Jeff Janowski.

Depictions of the Randall Library extension on the campus of UNCW.

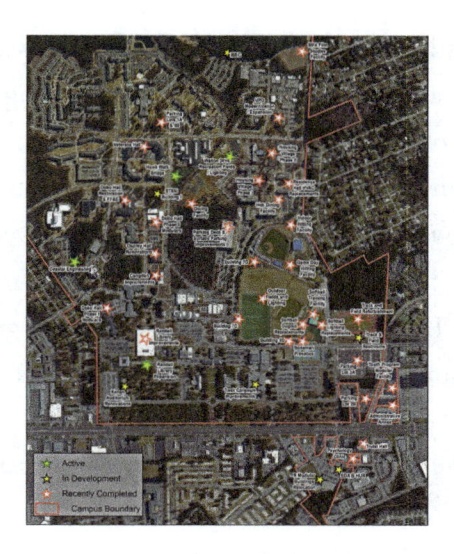

A map of the UNCW campus showing the construction projects of the strategic plan, 2015–2022.

Eventually, UNCW will need to expand again and fortunately, there's room for such growth. We still have about 200 unused acres on the campus property—although roughly half of it is environmentally protected—and we have been gifted 200 acres in Brunswick County and 700 acres along the I-40 highway on the way to Raleigh.

The success we experienced with the strategic plan didn't come without its challenges, though. Two years into it, the first of two unexpected events took place, which tested our resiliency, steadfastness, and ability to pull together and work hard.

Hurricane Florence

On September 14–16, 2018, Hurricane Florence hit Wilmington and UNCW head-on.

We watched the weather reports closely and when it intensified to a Category 5, we evacuated everyone from the campus, sending students home or to storm shelters. It downgraded slightly to a Category 4 and stalled as it hit land, hovering over us for an extended period of time. The winds packed a punch, damaging even the largest trees and a great proportion of roofs, but the biggest threat turned out to be water accumulation—the city received close to thirty inches of rain in two days. Normally, Wilmington receives fifty-five inches per year. The devastation throughout the region was significant and the financial impact on the university was immense: $134 million dollars.

The emergency operations center on campus remained open throughout the storm and dealt with the crisis as it happened. The rest of my team and I returned to campus as soon as possible. We were hindered by the many primary roads that were closed throughout the tri-county region due to flooding, washouts, and downed power lines and trees. The airport remained closed as well. For weeks our campus and all of Wilmington relied heavily on the New Hanover County emergency officials, who worked around the clock to conduct rescues, offer food and shelter, and resolve supply chain issues. Our general administrators worked closely with the community and state authorities to facilitate the students' safe return to campus and immediately upon their arrival, many of them offered assistance to Wilmingtonians in need.

As feared, our campus infrastructure was significantly impacted. Dobo Hall, which housed most of our chemistry and biology labs, suffered devastating flooding on both floors after the wind destroyed part of the roof. It took us two years to restore the building at a cost of $53 million from insurance funds. The consolation was that we received a modern, intelligent building we wouldn't have had otherwise.

Dobo Hall, second-story hallway impact before and after renovation. Photo credits: Jeff Janowski.

Dobo Hall roof impact before and after renovation. Photo credits: Mark Morgan.

In addition, thirteen of our small student apartment buildings, each of them housing thirty to forty students, had to be demolished due to damage and mold contamination. In their place, we constructed a student village comprised of four buildings holding 1,814 beds. This was accomplished through a public-private partnership (P3) with American College Facilities, a nonprofit organization that builds these types of apartments for universities around the country. The P3 prevented us from having to secure a sizable loan with 5–6 percent interest per year, an important factor since we already had $230 million of debt. Instead, we pay a monthly mortgage to American College Facilities and in forty years, the student village will officially become the property of UNCW.

Despite the vast amount of damage the campus experienced, students and staff worked and advocated together, critical funds were secured, academic schedules were normalized within four weeks, and renovations advanced so that by early 2020, life was getting back to normal.

Groundbreaking ceremony for the student village, 2019.

The completed P3 Student Village on UNCW's campus, 2021.
Photo credit: Jeff Janowski.

Lessons from the Catastrophe

- Diversify one's risks; do not build most of the labs in one science building.
- Harden roofs and build for the worst (135 mph wind speed, not just 100 mph).

- Keep the emergency-response team ready and well equipped. It pays off. We were enormously assisted by our sister universities in the system, who sent personnel to assist on-site immediately following the storm.
- Prioritize and continually test the efficiency of communication systems throughout the campus.
- Celebrate the ways students and staff pitch in with their time and efforts to assist with the cleanup.
- Understand the importance of the continuity of graduation; do everything necessary to ensure the seniors will graduate on time.

COVID-19 Pandemic

Just as we were returning to normal after Hurricane Florence, we were hit by the COVID-19 pandemic. Who would have thought that almost one hundred years after the Spanish flu the world would be facing another worldwide pandemic? New phrases and words became important parts of our daily lexicon, such as upsurge, de-densification, and hybrid classes.

Students were sent home on March 23, 2020, as America entered lockdown, attending classes remotely for the remainder of the spring and summer semesters. We then put together a large team led by Dr. Charles Hardy, the dean of the College of Health and Human Services, that led us forward according to the guidelines put forth by the state's Department of Health (DOH), local DOH, and the Centers for Disease Control and Prevention (CDC).

The "Back to the Nest" campaign in the fall of 2020 emphasized the 3 Ws: wear a mask, wash your hands, and watch your distance. We selected 150 beds in Galloway Hall as a place for isolation and quarantine as students gradually returned and classes resumed. Students had the option of attending classes in person, online, or a hybrid of the two. When an upsurge in cases emerged, we had to de-densify our dorms again, sending 800–900 students back home and only allowing one person per dorm room on campus.

In the spring of 2021, vaccines became available. The COVID vaccines were approved without any major clinical trial because of the urgent need around the world; in one year, pharmaceutical companies were able to develop, manufacture, and receive FDA approval instead of it taking the typical five to ten years. At this time, we also received monies from the federal government to help students pay for activities and fees.

Fall 2021 saw us trying to come back to normal, but the Delta variant forced us to retrench again. We increased COVID testing (up to four thousand tests a week), continued our isolation/quarantine procedures, and offered vaccinations. No one at all could have predicted the effect that COVID would have on study-abroad programs and international exchanges between universities. For many of the upperclassmen who graduated during the pandemic, their inability to study abroad was a profound disappointment. Hopefully, they will be willing and able to explore new countries and grow an international network of peers in their careers.

It was impossible to please everyone. Some people were saying we needed to close the university while others were saying "No, we've got to open up more." I focused on the main purpose of the university, which was to teach and educate students while following government-imposed mandates.

It was a very stressful time. Everyone was getting maniacal because of the pandemic and divisive over lockdowns and face masks.

Face masks in particular became a huge issue. I heard from parents all the time who said, "Why are you making my child wear face masks? When she comes home, I immediately tell her to take off the face mask. But you're telling her that to go to class or to work, she has to wear a mask." I had to explain that the majority of professors would not teach if we didn't require students to wear a face mask. I understood both sides, but ultimately, wearing a face mask was not going to kill anyone.

In the spring of 2022, my last semester as chancellor, we largely succeeded in operating on a fairly normal (prepandemic) basis. We were even able to provide all employees (faculty and staff alike) with a salary increase of 2.5 percent on top of the 2.5 percent provided by the state. In addition, we resumed graduation ceremonies on campus, but graduates were only allowed to bring one guest.

Both Hurricane Florence and the pandemic could have derailed our strategic plan. Yet, despite it all, we were able to maintain our vision and achieve our goals. We were very constrained in what we could do, but we continued to grow. The university's courageous actions allowed us to become the fastest-growing university in the system, which allowed us to receive additional funding from the legislature.

Surprise Achievements

A New Classification

Because the university had continued to grow in both enrollment and research activity, the Carnegie Classification of Institutions of Higher Education (CCIHE) reclassified UNCW in 2019 from a regional university to a doctoral university—high research activity R2. This bump up in classification was unplanned and a very pleasant shock; it was something I had wanted to attain, but I left it out of the strategic plan because I could not risk that level of unpredictability.

Every three years, the CCIHE compares and classifies all U.S. higher education institutions according to various criteria. For instance, to become classified as an R1—the highest classification—it requires producing at least fifty doctorates in any specialty plus approximately $100 million of research a year. In comparison, R2 classification only requires a minimum of twenty doctorates a year and $5 million of research.

Thus, the more independent research a school conducts, the more funding they receive from the two major funding arms of the federal government: the National Science Foundation and the National Institutes of Health. Each of these organizations distributes $30–$40 billion a year to all the research universities in the country. UNC Chapel Hill, as one of the top research universities in the nation, receives about $1 billion a year from these organizations to further its research. All the other NC schools get a lot less than that. For example, UNC Charlotte gets about $52 million and UNCW about $20 million.

With this in mind, we worked hard to hire quality professors capable of submitting research projects that required $500,000–$2 million or more to complete. The funding is important to the professors since they get promoted on the basis of what they publish, and to publish anything of significance, they need to conduct quality research. And the funding is important to the school since a portion of it can be used to buy better equipment, improve programs, and construct new buildings. It's a win-win situation for everyone involved.

The caveat is that a university can be downgraded if it doesn't maintain CCIHE standards. Therefore, universities work very hard to retain their status and the associated funds. But our goal wasn't just to maintain R2 status; we wanted to work toward R1 status. Toward that effort, we added four new PhD programs to our existing two and continued to hire quality professors. I believe UNCW can become an R1 school, but it will require us to at least double the number of our PhD programs.

Since obtaining R2 classification, UNCW has become one of four universities in the UNC system to consistently appear in the *Fiske Guide to Colleges*, and in the 2021/2022 school year, it ranked as one of the top 100 best public universities in the country, according to *U.S. News and World Report.*

A painting by James Tennison that served as my official portrait as chancellor of UNCW, which hangs in the Gallery of Chancellors at Alderman Hall, 2022.

A Long-Awaited Program

One program that UNCW had been trying to introduce since the 2007/2008 academic year was engineering—one of the leading disciplines in this country. Simply put, if you don't have engineering, you're missing out. However, opposition from other schools blocked our initial efforts to add this specialty to our academic roster. To combat the situation, I determined that UNCW would stop vying for traditional engineering programs and instead set ourselves apart by launching the first coastal engineering program in the country.

My first step was to approach NC State with my noncompete solution. After some negotiations, they agreed and I submitted my request to the Board of Governors. Their prompt approval was an unexpected and welcome event. I had been confident that we would add the program, but I didn't know how long the approval process might take so I didn't include it in the strategic plan.

Construction soon began on the new facility, and we imported a sophisticated simulation tank from Great Britain capable of reproducing the various coastal environments of the United States. The program officially opened to students in 2018 and by December 2022, UNCW had awarded the inaugural class of seventeen students with their bachelor's degree in coastal engineering.

During this time, I also obtained approval to create a second engineering program in intelligence systems, which includes software development, cybersecurity, and artificial intelligence. It launched in the fall of 2023.

I did not push for these engineering programs just for the heck of it; I pushed because there's a demand for them and they enabled us to significantly increase our research funding. Our nursing, allied health, and computer science programs also continued to receive research funding. And, by effectively arguing that aquaculture is indeed a form of agriculture, we received money for our marine science program.

If you're not thinking creatively for the future, you're not going to successfully meet your goals.

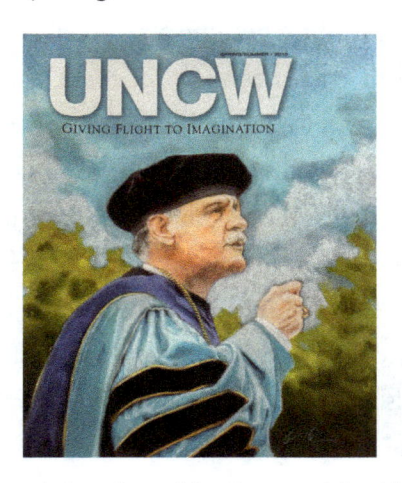

An artist's rendering of me giving the speech in which I coined the phrase "Giving Flight to Imagination," which became UNCW's motto. *UNCW* magazine, spring/summer issue, 2016.

The Impact of Social Media

When I worked in the pharmaceutical industry, Internet was around, but it wasn't pervasive in the workplace. At Lilly and BMS, as suppliers of pharmaceutical products and medical devices, we were constantly interfacing with doctors and, to a lesser degree, pharmacists. We did not have a lot of contact with the public. At J&J, we added consumer products such as Tylenol® and mouthwash, which we did sell directly to the general public. But during that time, if people had an issue, they tended to send a letter or a private email to us. It took a bit of time and effort, which made people think more about what they were going to say.

Then came the explosive growth of social media, particularly such platforms as Facebook and Twitter. Social media allowed an individual's complaint or accusation toward companies—and their executives—to reach a global audience in seconds. One negative comment bred a host of them; trolling became a real challenge.

This extended to emails as well. As chancellor, I often received emails regarding an issue someone had about something on campus. That was fine; I welcomed different viewpoints and constructive criticism. But many times, these emails contained unfounded accusations and inappropriate comments, which were then shared online to thousands of other people who had no affiliation or direct involvement with the university or the issue at hand. As a result, I was inundated with copycat emails from across the country and around the world.

By 2020, I was scanning hundreds of emails a day, most of them filled with terribly offensive and coarse language. They threatened, they diminished, and they used the worst terms possible. It was pathetic. For each message, I had to determine whether it was best to respond and if so, how to do so in a legally protected way.

Yes, the Internet and social media have driven globalization through advertisements and things like that, which is a good thing for companies and universities; brand recognition is important and helps us share information about our products and services to attract new clients and students. But in many other ways, the Internet and social media have opened up a whole new, huge can of worms.

Many doctors, for example, are challenged by the Internet. Patients come into the exam room demanding prescriptions they've seen advertised for their self-diagnosed ailments. This places doctors in a tough situation. They may not be aware of the requested new drug because a pharmaceutical sales rep hasn't yet met with them to inform them of the product, or maybe the drug hasn't even been released in the U.S. yet. Even if they are familiar with the drug, doctors don't want to blindly prescribe it; they want to examine the patient and make informed decisions based on their medical training and experience, not what the Internet has to say.

The Internet has made our lives more complex, a little more complicated, and fast-paced. Everyone wants immediate results ... and many of them want a refund if they're unhappy with something.

Social media has been good to its founders who have made a ton of money from it, but it has become a challenge for almost everyone else, particularly executives and administrators who are forced to occupy their time on things that have no meaningful impact. I once had a boss who said, "Never worry about things you cannot control. If you engage in things you cannot control, you're in trouble." He was totally correct.

But it's not just companies that have been negatively impacted by the Internet. Employees, too, have struggled, particularly those who have commingled their private and public activities online to the detriment of their work. One of the biggest, and saddest, examples of this concerned one of our faculty members, professor Michael Adams.

Standing for Free Speech

When I first arrived on campus in July 2015, many people warned me that I had a tough professor to deal with—Michael Adams. Several years prior, Dr. Adams had challenged the university over a denial of his promotion to full professor by taking them to court. He won and even collected back pay and legal fee reimbursement.

My first major contact with him took place after Donald Trump's presidential campaign stop on campus in August 2016. One of our students protested the candidate in a way that prompted the Secret Service to intervene. It so happened that the student was from Sudan and was also a gay black Muslim woman, which prompted Michael Adams to talk about her on his blog.

His posts triggered a campus-wide firestorm. The university's administrators and faculty were outraged by his behavior, and students publicly protested. I received tons of emails from the entire Wilmington area urging me to fire him immediately. But I believe in free speech.

Did I agree with what he said? No, I did not. But he wrote those things on his own personal computer in the privacy of his own home. In the classroom, he kept his opinions to himself and was a great educator. In fact, one young lady stood up in the middle of a meeting that I was facilitating about the matter with approximately seventy students and said, "I have had this professor for two semesters. He's given everyone the opportunity to speak up. He has never commented about politics of any kind in the classroom, ever. I don't think he should be fired." She had a lot of courage to do that, and she faced a lot of criticism from her peers afterward.

The provost and I met with Dr. Adams. I pointed out the unfairness of an adult professor targeting a student and said, "I'm working very hard to bring students into your classroom and you're making every effort to make sure they leave. This is not going to work. You've got to stop." And he did stop targeting students. However, he continued to post his opinions about hot-button topics and how they applied to our campus.

His behavior and the vehemency of his posts intensified over the years. By late spring 2020, the Black Lives Matter social justice movement was sweeping the country and he was prepared to do battle with them.

In June, he called me and asked for an online (virtual) meeting. I invited one of my deans to join us, and we were surprised when he spontaneously asked about early retirement. He explained that even though he had been with the university for twenty-six years and had planned to work another four years, he was receiving death threats and he wanted out. Would we be willing to provide a settlement of some sort? The answer was yes.

After he departed the university, I expected him to lead some far-right group and speak nationally to his following. Instead, two weeks later, on July 23, 2020, he killed himself. Despite being a good professor, his passionate involvement in politics ended in tragedy. Even his inclusion in our campus memorial garden ceremony was controversial, which his family and friends attended in honor of him and all the other students and staff who passed away that year.

Immediately, my inbox was flooded with emails accusing me of being responsible for his death. It seemed as though every single far-right individual in Wilmington, throughout North Carolina, and across the USA accused me of killing him. I felt that we had treated him fairly and had defended his right to free speech successfully, but they felt that we had put too much pressure on him, which forced him to resign and led to his own demise. This was not the case.

Look, I am a person who lost a brother to suicide. I could never understand what led him to do that. I also spent a good part of my career selling antidepressants to doctors and pharmacies for people to take so they wouldn't commit suicide. I stood up for Dr. Adams's right to free speech, but he was responsible for his own decisions and actions.

Why am I such a strong supporter of freedom of speech? Because I have lived in a country that did not pay attention to it. Between 1964 and 1985, Brazil was under a military dictatorship that did not allow us to speak out against them. When I was in college, we quickly learned not to say anything negative about the government. If we did, we could be identified and picked up by the military police. If such a person was lucky, they would simply be arrested; if they were unlucky, they would disappear. So you can't tell me that freedom of speech isn't critical to uphold. Freedom of speech is fundamental for democracy.

Many of my critics said none of that mattered; that Michael Adams should have been prohibited from blogging. My response was, "So it was okay in the 1960s for the students in places like Berkeley and Princeton to rebel against the establishment under the protection of free speech, but now anyone who disagrees with your point of view is to be oppressed? You cannot do that. Freedom of speech is fundamental for everyone."

Although my stance led many people to dislike me, my actions helped the college attain green status with the Foundation for Individual Rights and Expression. This organization determines how well a college or university defends free speech and assigns them a color status: red (worst), yellow, or green (best). When I first became chancellor, we were at red; when I left, we had become green. This was an accomplishment that greatly pleased all of us.

The Social Justice Movement

Spring and summer of 2020 saw substantial disquiet amid our African American student population because of Dr. Adams's blogging activities. By that fall, black students, faculty, and alumni presented a list of needs to be addressed regarding the university's reaction to not only his actions, but also the larger social justice movement that had swept the country following the murder of George Floyd in Minneapolis that May.

Noting the heated climate and growing racial tensions as students returned to campus post-COVID, I organized the Renewal and Change Accountability Committee comprised of black students, faculty, and alumni to address the needs that had been identified by our students and faculty of color.

One of their complaints was that my cabinet and I were silent on certain issues; they wanted us to communicate more. Specifically, they wanted us to speak out against every act of violence that happened to minorities across the country. However, my belief was that unless events directly affected Wilmington or UNCW specifically, we would not publicly speak to the issues. We shouldn't take it upon ourselves to resolve all the issues of the world.

In addition, my position as chancellor required me to serve our entire student population, not just specific groups on campus. I made it clear I believed all lives mattered. I publicly stated that UNCW served a variety of races and ethnicities and each deserved the same constitutional rights. I was vilified, but I refused to act as though we lived in North Korea.

In response, they went to the power of the Internet and distributed a questionnaire for people to vote on my resignation or termination. Talk about cancel culture. It was crazy. I came to this country because I wanted to live in a democratic society, one where people had the ability to express themselves. But now, many citizens find that if they express too much, they can be challenged and even prosecuted.

I did see the validity of many of their other requests, though, and we worked with the Office of Diversity and Inclusion to strengthen our dedicated centers—places where students can engage with the university and also assert their identity, so to speak. These centers were the Upperman African American Cultural Center, the Centro Hispano, and the Mohin-Scholz LGBTQIA Resource Office. I also approved an Asian Center that will be established soon.

During my time there, I worked with the Campus Climate Task Force to pursue ten different initiatives that made UNCW more diverse and inclusive. In addition, the university committed to spend $1.5 million per year for five years to offer equitable representation at the undergraduate and graduate levels, to seek out and hire more faculty of color, to increase training against racism, and to create inclusive conditions for all students.

The feedback from students about all these efforts was positive.

Winning Seasons

The athletic director, the various athletic personnel, and I worked together to pursue three clear objectives for the athletics department as a whole: it must be academically proficient as measured by Academic Progress Rate, league competitive (post-season tournaments), and financially sound. On all three counts, UNCW athletics is making progress as it supports an extensive number of men's and women's sports.

The UNCW baseball team has a well-deserved reputation for excellence, and Kathy and I enjoyed attending their games; there are few places more pleasant than a sunny afternoon at Brooks Field. The biggest draw at UNCW, though, is men's basketball, which offers an unequaled experience in Trask Auditorium.

Prior to 2015, UNCW had qualified for the NCAA March Madness tournament four times, which is a good record for a university of our size. However, under the leadership of coach Kevin Keatts, we got to participate two more times during my tenure. In the 2015/2016 season, we won the Colonial Athletic Association (CAA) tournament and played an early round of March Madness against Duke, the previous year's national champion. We finished ahead of them in the first half but eventually lost, 93–85. In the 2016/2017 season, we once again became CAA champions and entered March Madness. We lost to Virginia, 76–71, who went on to win the national championship that year. In 2021/2022, our new coach, Takayo Siddle, led us to a championship regular season and a spot at the College Basketball Invitational in Daytona Beach, Florida. We won the tournament, beating Middle Tennessee State University (96–90) in an exciting game with two overtimes.

One of my favorite end-of-year events was the sashing ceremony for the graduating student athletes. The white sash they received at this ceremony was worn at commencement, along with any cords they may have earned for their academic, leadership, and membership accomplishments during their time on campus. All of these served as visible symbols of the special ways in which students excelled during their years at UNCW.

It was wonderful to celebrate with the team after UNCW won the game to become CAA Champions (I'm in the middle row, second from right), 2016.

Kenan House and the Azalea Festival

The staff at UNCW ensured the chancellor's residence at the corner of Market and 17th Streets in downtown Wilmington looked pristine and meticulously cared for at all times. The longtime housekeeper, Ms. Sandra Rowell, kept Kenan House in an impeccable, graceful state while the gardeners maintained the manicured grounds year-round, making it one of North Carolina's most beautiful private gardens. Over the years, I spoke with many people about the fascinating history of the Kenan family and the house and collected books on the subject matter, too.

Kenan House, the official residence of UNCW chancellors, Wilmington, NC, mid-2010s.

In 2016, the Kenan House and the Wise Alumni House next door were part of the Cape Fear Garden Club's Azalea Festival Garden Tour, which was an honor. Kathy and I participated in all its associated events and stayed in the garden to speak with people on the tour. A few years later, the festival's Garden Tour Belle Tea was held at the residence, at which more than one hundred Azalea Belles (later renamed Garden Ambassadors) enjoyed tea with their mothers and grandmothers. These young women had been selected to represent their schools and their city throughout the week-long Azalea Festival activities.

On Saturday, April 14, 2018, Kathy and I were invited to join members of the UNCW dance team and Sammy the Seahawk aboard the UNCW float during the annual Azalea Festival Parade in downtown Wilmington. Our float was beautifully decorated, featuring lots of teal (our school color) and a rainbow. Prominently featured throughout the parade were azalea flowers and Garden Ambassadors wearing pink, yellow, or green dresses. Young children did cartwheels on the sidelines and seated spectators stood and clapped as our float approached. It was very clear to me how much the community respects its university. Kathy and I enjoyed being in this remarkable event; it was one of the most memorable things I did as chancellor.

Kathy and I with two of the Azalea Belles (Garden Ambassadors) and their mothers on the grounds of Kenan House, 2019.

I pose with the UNCW dance team at the Azalea Festival Parade, Wilmington, NC, March 14, 2018. Photo credit: Jeff Janowski.

Key Relationships

Many professors made a memorable impression on me. One was Dr. Thomas Simpson and his wife, Cindy, who invited international students to their home each Thanksgiving to enjoy a traditional turkey dinner and learn about the holiday's history. Dr. Richard Shew was a wonderful steward of our natural habitat on campus, particularly the longleaf pine trees. Dr. Ron Vetter showed me how quality faculty leadership can propel new programs. Other standouts include Dr. Dylan McNamara, the creator of our new coastal engineering program, and Dr. Mark Lammers, who took our data science program to great heights.

A number of professors provided me with an autographed copy of their published books while they were hot off the press and others invited me to their end-of-summer gatherings for their departments. Several professors, when seeing me walk along the campus pathways, would approach to tell me they agreed with me on certain issues. Their support mattered enormously to me.

Kathy and I stroll along UNCW's Chancellor's Walk.

In addition to faculty members, several other individuals were vital to my success at UNCW. Dr. Katrin Wesner-Harts was an exceptional steward of everyone's health on campus during the pandemic, keeping us on track with testing, vaccines, and the supply chain. Former chancellor James Leutze met me for lunch at his convenience to share ideas, and Thomas Kenan, the namesake of the chancellor's residence, was a longtime supporter of UNCW, particularly the marine science program. I valued my time with both these gentlemen.

I'm joined by Tom Kenan (the house's namesake, center) and Vice-Chancellor Eddie Stuart (far right) at a reception at Kenan House.

Another cherished relationship was with Dr. Richard Morrison, a former colleague at Eli Lilly who had retired to Wilmington. He and his wife, Belinda, were Kathy's and my only acquaintances upon our arrival in town, and our friendship strengthened through regular meaningful discussions. He was actively involved with UNCW, where he worked as a professor, was involved with the international MBA program, and served as a longtime mentor to students in the business school on campus.

Dr. Richard Morrison and I after one of our meaningful discussions, 2022.

And finally, meeting with the fellow university presidents at the Colonial Athletic Association (CAA) was always interesting as well. Our commissioner, Joe D'Antonio, was ever-present at these events, speaking the right words at the right time.

Personal Achievements

Power 100 - The State's Most Influential Leaders
Recognition makes us feel good, and I can say that my twelve years in academia generated some greatly appreciated acknowledgments. These wonderful recognitions were humbling and made me even more willing to serve. For my five years at West Virginia, I was named a "Distinguished Mountaineer" by the Governor of the State, Earl Ray Tomblin. Also in 2015, West Virginia's *State Journal* included me in the "Who's Who in West Virginia Business."

In North Carolina, the *Greater Wilmington Business Journal* included me in their "Wilmington Biz 100" not just once, but three times (2019, 2020, and 2021). In the spring of 2020, *Business North Carolina* included me in their "Power 100: The State's Most Influential Leaders" issue in the educational category.

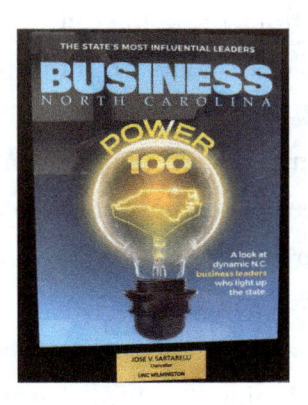

The plaque I received to commemorate being included as one of the one hundred best leaders in the state of North Carolina, 2020.

I continued my community involvement by holding positions of leadership with the Wilmington Chamber of Commerce, the Rotary Club downtown, and the NC Biotechnology Center. I spoke each year to the Wilmington Senior Club and at various county/city events to promote UNCW's Osher Lifelong Learning Institute to adults within our community.

I was also involved with key organizations in the region such as the Port of Wilmington, Wilmington International Airport (where I helped successfully bring a third carrier to town), and the Wilmington Business Development Board, which helps attract new businesses to the region. Other groups I worked with in North Carolina included Higher Education Works, Campus Compact, and the Board of Governors' Task Forces.

Sartarelli Hall

Perhaps the greatest recognition bestowed on me was the naming of one of the campus buildings as Sartarelli Hall by UNCW's Board of Trustees. Sartarelli Hall was previously identified as Osprey Hall and is located across from the Cameron School of Business. The building houses the departments of anthropology, mathematics, and physics.

When I was leaving UNCW, the president of the UNC system said, "Zito, of the sixteen chancellors I have, you are one of the best." How is it possible? I'm not a professor. The only teaching I did was while I was earning my PhD at Michigan State. The answer is that I was willing to face challenges and put in the work.

From the very beginning, I wanted to make UNCW a doctoral university and introduce engineering programs. Achieving both those goals led to the university being ranked as one of the top one hundred best public universities in the country. I believe that creativity, persistence, and hard work will continue to keep UNCW at such laudable heights.

Announcement of Sartarelli Hall on the campus of UNCW, April 2022. Photo credit: Jeff Janowski.

Kathy and I standing outside the newly minted Sartarelli Hall, April 2022. Photo credit: Jeff Janowski.

Order of the Long Leaf Pine

This award was created in 1963 to honor individuals who have provided high levels of service to the state and their communities.

I was humbled by my friends and colleagues who nominated me for this significant recognition. On April 28, 2022, Governor Roy Cooper bestowed upon me the plaque and inducted me as an "Ambassador Extraordinary" with the special privilege of proposing the following North Carolina toast (as it appears on my plaque):

"Here's to the land of the long leaf pine,
The summer land where the sun doth shine,
Where the weak grow strong and the strong grow great,
Here's to 'down home,' the Old North State!"[45]

My Order of the Long Leaf Pine certificate, awarded to me in spring 2022.

---

45 From the original poem "The Old North State" by Lenora Monteiro Martin in 1904. For the history of the poem, visit https://www.ncpedia.org/symbols/toast (last accessed October 17, 2023). For the history of the Order of the Long Leaf Pine, visit https://longleafpinesociety.org/anthem/ (last accessed October 17, 2023).

Personal Affairs

Bypass

On most weekends, Kathy and I went to Wrightsville Beach where we walked along the sand, enjoying the sun and sea breeze. In the fall of 2017, the walks became less enjoyable for me as I increasingly grew fatigued and felt some chest discomfort. I made an appointment with a cardiologist who concluded that I needed at least one stent. However, the procedure couldn't be completed since the arteries were too clogged. I was shocked, as my family had no history of cardiovascular problems. However, I had experienced a lot of stress throughout my career and maintained a diet rich in fat.

A bypass was scheduled locally until one of my friends on the Board of Trustees urged me to do it at Duke, which is known as the best hospital in the state. I used her connections and underwent a successful quadruple bypass surgery there on January 30, 2018 (which made the second page of the Wilmington newspaper!). Unable to work for at least a month, I spent much of my time doing outpatient rehab at New Hanover Regional Medical Center. Family and friends came to visit, and I saved all the cards that were sent to me by the kind people of Wilmington. By the time I was cleared to go back to work, my energy levels were up, I was once again enjoying walks, and I had begun eating a modified diet.

I was happy to return to the beach, 2018. Photo credit: Jeff Janowski.

Retirement

In 2021, I began to think about retirement. When I broached the subject to the Board of Trustees and the Board of Governors, they asked me to consider staying on as chancellor for a full ten-year term. But after the tsunami of challenges I had recently dealt with, I decided that I would retire the following year (2022). I had never committed to a certain tenure, so I believed seven years was a respectable amount of time to serve as chancellor.

Kathy and I discussed our options and decided we would relocate to Naples, Florida. I had some ideas of what I might want to pursue next, but for the first time in my life, I didn't leave one position to enter directly into another.

I was ready to give flight to my imagination in new, exciting ways and looked forward to what awaited me in the future.

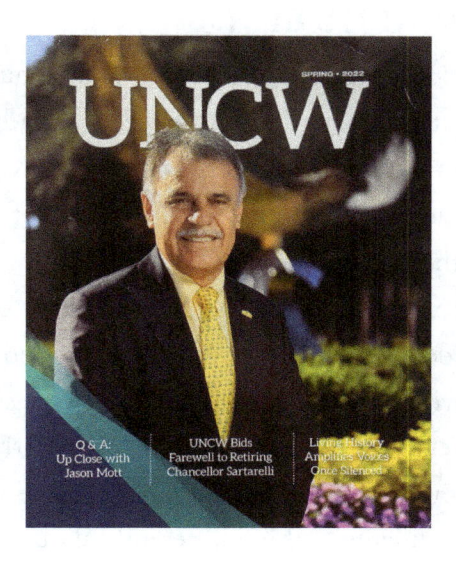

I was honored by a feature article about my retirement in *UNCW* magazine, spring 2022.

Losses

On March 11, 2014, I lost Lonnie Bell, my American father. I had brought him and his second wife, Anne, to visit us in Morgantown, West Virginia, which they enjoyed. Lonnie was a man of many talents, was patient, hardworking, fully dedicated to family, and had an ever-present sense of humor. Throughout his life, farming had dealt him some tough blows, but he was resilient and persevered.

On July 6, 2022, my eldest sister Maria Aparecida ("Cidinha"), the one who worked hard to teach me my first letters as a young boy, passed away. She continues to be profoundly missed by all of us, but especially by her daughter, Conceicao, and her grandson, Bruno, who would have loved to have her attend his graduation where he will receive a PhD in materials science.

IMAGINATION AT ITS BEST

These "Imagination at its Best" summaries have sought to identify things done "out of the ordinary" in order to advance a cause, a project, or an initiative. The initiatives always represented an innovation—something very different. Indeed, a jolt of imagination to follow a new path.

"The Academy at Last" chapter speaks about education from the lenses of student and provider. I have not proposed a new path but merely reaffirmed a path that is essential for the survival of a free society. The university in a free society serves as a marketplace of ideas and should accommodate different opinions, open doors to imagination, and enable students to think differently about the future.

We remain free to do all this by adhering to, emphasizing, and living out the First Amendment of the U.S. Constitution:

> **AMMENDMENTS TO THE CONSTITUTION OF THE UNITED STATES OF AMERICA: AMENDMENT 1**
>
> **"Congress shall make no law respecting an establishment of religion, or prohibiting the free exercise thereof; or abridging the freedom of speech, or of the press; or the right of the people peaceably to assemble, and to petition the Government for a redress of grievances."**

Back in the late 1960s and early 1970s when I was living in Brazil, I lived under a military regime where freedom of speech was instantly eliminated. My family and I had been accustomed to saying whatever came to mind, but then, suddenly, we had to guard our words and shield our thoughts. Speech became nuanced as we carefully chose words to speak in public that would not fall into some banned category. It was difficult to do, and it impressed upon us the importance of free speech as the foundation of democratic life. Without it, one cannot speak of democracy.

From 1980 to 2010, when I worked for three major multinational pharmaceutical companies in a variety of countries, I never felt constrained in exercising free speech. But from 2010 to 2022 while working on U.S. soil, I experienced attacks against free speech. I realized how different the world was becoming and how important it was to defend freedom of speech at UNCW.

When I was officially installed as chancellor of UNCW, I swore to defend the Constitution of the United States and the Constitution of North Carolina and therefore, I explicitly stated that I would defend the various amendments of those documents.

As we move forward, we have to take a strong position to defend free speech because once that is gone, democracy will go with it. All of us will have lost a free society.

The Big Picture

2010–2023 Overview

WORLD / U.S. [46]

- Dow: 10,428.05[47]–33,127.28,[48] +318%
- Haiti experiences a devastating earthquake in 2010
- Osama bin Laden is killed by U.S. soldiers, Gaddafi is killed, and South Sudan splits from Sudan in 2011
- Paris Agreement recharges concerns about climate change
- Russia annexes Crimea in 2014
- Same-sex marriage is legalized in the U.S. in 2015
- U.S. presidency moves from Obama to Trump in 2016
- Arab Spring protests lead to revolutions in Tunisia, Egypt, and Bahrain; ISIS/ISIL grows their presence in Syria and Iraq
- UK votes to leave the EU in 2016; officially departs in 2020
- Occupy Wall Street protest takes place over the financial crisis
- Migrant crisis in Europe
- Smartphones are widespread and 5G networks launch
- Me Too women's movement starts
- Edward Snowden seeks refugee status in Russia; becomes Russian citizen in 2022
- Cable comes under pressure from streaming services like Netflix; streamers also come under pressure by end of 2022

---

46 Source of historical data in this section: "2010s," Wikimedia Foundation, https://en.wikipedia.org/wiki/2010s and "2020s," Wikimedia Foundation, https://en.wikipedia.org/wiki/2020s. Last accessed September 26, 2023.

47 Source of the Dow range in this section: "Dow Jones Industrial Average," Wikimedia Foundation, https://en.wikipedia.org/wiki/Dow_Jones_Industrial_Average. Last accessed October 24, 2023.

48 Source of the Dow: "How major US stock indexes fared Friday, 10/20/2023," AP News, https://apnews.com/article/financial-markets-stocks-dow-nasdaq-1c7838aecb57ef010b13c01877571bf2. Last accessed October 24, 2023.

- China transforms into superpower
- COVID-19 global pandemic strikes; more than 1 million people die in U.S., more than 680,000 in Brazil
- George Floyd's death leads to the Black Lives Matter (BLM) movement—cancels "All Lives Matter"
- Russia invades Ukraine in 2022

BRAZIL

- Luiz Inácio Lula da Silva, Dilma Rousseff, Michel Temer, Jair Bolsonaro
- The Operation (Lava Jato), led by Sergio Moro, aggressively pursues corruption in federal government
- Mismanagement of federal accounts leads to Dilma Rousseff's impeachment
- Petrobras and Brazil's National Bank of Economic and Social Development are implicated and suffer the pressure from Lula and his team
- Lula sentenced to twelve years in prison—only stays one-and-a-half years; is freed on a technicality
- Country stops growing
- Lula elected president

PERSONAL SIGNIFICANT EVENTS / ACHIEVEMENTS

- Lives in Hopewell, New Jersey; Morgantown, West Virginia; Wilmington, North Carolina; Naples, Florida

West Virginia University, Morgantown, West Virginia (2010–2015)
Milan Puskar Dean, College of Business and Economics

- Member, Enrollment Committee (2013–2015)

- Member, Senior Academic Administrator Personnel Committee (2013–2015)
- Member, Health Disparities Task Force (2012–2015)
- Member, Shale Gas Utilization Taskforce (2012–2015)
- Leader, Global Engagement Round Table (2010–2015)
- Member, the Economic Well-Being and Engagement Round Table (2010–2015)
- Member, Strategic Planning Council (2010–2015)
- Member, Research, Innovation, and Commercialization Task Force (2010–2015)
- Member, Search Committees for Deans and Vice Presidents and Five-Year Review Committee for Deans (2010–2015)
- Member, Council of Deans (2010–2015)
- Board and Finance Committee Member, West Virginia United Health System (2014–2015)
- Member, West Virginia Chamber of Commerce Education Task Force (2012–2015)
- Board and Executive Committee Member, Blanchette Rockefeller Neurosciences Institute, WVU (2012–2015)
- Board Member, Bio West Virginia (2011–2015)
- Member, Association to Advance Collegiate Schools of Business
- Member, Examining Team for the re-accreditation of Utah State University (fall 2012)

University of North Carolina Wilmington, Wilmington, North Carolina (2015–2022)

Chancellor

- Chairman, UNCW Cabinet (2015–2022)
- Member, UNCW Board of Trustees (2015–2022)

- Member Ex Officio, UNCW Foundation Board (2015-2022)
- Member Ex Officio, UNCW Endowment Board (2015-2022)
- Chairman, Watson College Foundation (2015-2022)
- Member, UNC Board of Governors' Audit, Risk Management, and Compliance Committee (2017-2018)
- Member, UNC Board of Governors' Educational Planning, Policies, and Programs (2017-2018)
- Member, UNC Board of Governors' System Performance Funding Task Force Member (2017-2018)
- UNC Board of Governors' Personnel and Tenure Committee (2018-2022)
- Member, UNC Board of Governors' Strategic Initiatives Committee (2018-2019)
- Member, UNC Board of Governors' Health Care Special Committee (2018-2019)
- Member, Rotary Club, Wilmington Downtown (2015-2022)
- Board Member, Wilmington Chamber of Commerce (2015-2022)
- Board Member, North Carolina Biotechnology Center (2016-2023)

LOSSES

- Joáo Carlos "Carlito" Sartarelli, March 14, 2010
- Lonnie Bell, March 11, 2014
- Maria Aparecida "Cidinha" Sartarelli, July 6, 2022

8

IMAGINATION AT ITS BEST

> "Imagination is more important than knowledge. Knowledge is limited. Imagination encircles the world."
>
> **ALBERT EINSTEIN**[49]

As the decades of my life unfolded, I came to recognize that imagination was the crux of each of my major life events. But with imagination comes risk. Imagination is the spark that attracts people, but risk is the element that often prevents them from taking action. While differentiation brings disruption, resiliency can ultimately bring about a better situation. This has proven true over and over again in my own life.

Imagination pulled the strings so that my brothers were able to create a new future for themselves and our entire family through tomatoes. When they started out with just an idea and initiated action,

---

[49] George Sylvester Viereck, "What Life Means to Einstein," *The Saturday Evening Post*, October 26, 1929; 117. https://www.saturdayeveningpost.com/wp-content/uploads/satevepost/what_life_means_to_einstein.pdf. Last accessed October 24, 2023.

there was a real risk of losing everything our family had attained up to that point; there was no way of knowing if it was going to be successful until they completed the first growing season. But along with the triumph of that first season came the unexpected loss of family relationships. Nevertheless, their imagination led to a much better situation for us all.

The second example of imagination at its best was when I took the chance on AFS. It seems so innocuous to be an exchange student today, but in the context of the mid-1960s in a small town in Brazil's interior, it was an uncommon idea. Many people, including my father, thought it was a crazy thing to do. Nevertheless, my family helped me gather $95 that I placed in my pocket the day I traveled to Dimmitt, Texas, knowing there was a real risk my U.S. course credits might not be accepted by Brazil upon my return and I might have to repeat a year of school.

In fact, I had to complete four more months of high school in Brazil before I was officially recognized as a high school graduate and allowed to take the university examinations. But the upsides of the AFS experience far outweighed the extra class work. I learned a new language that helped me pay for college, developed greater confidence to face the world and its challenges, made incredible friends, and started to think beyond school. The triumph of AFS superseded all the disruptions and ultimately led me to attend the best business school in Brazil.

The third example of imagination at its best was "Triumph through Scholarships." Would I have done everything I have done without scholarships, starting with the AFS one? Probably not. The scholarships brought expectations and responsibility, which enabled me to break through the despair and sense of overwhelm that initially set in as I transitioned from living in Ribeirão Bonito (a town of six thousand inhabitants) to São Paulo (a city of approximately twelve million) without much money and living with three other young men from my hometown. Incredibly, they never tried to collect a penny from me for rent! They were so proud of my studies that they were willing to have me stay with them for free.

The financial help from Dona Deo and Dr. Antonio enabled me to attend Getulio Vargas—it was a scholarship out of the goodness of their hearts. The Fulbright Scholarship (with funds from the General Electric Foundation) enabled me to return to the United States to attend Michigan State University for my MBA, and finally, I was financially able to obtain my PhD through two MSU assistantships augmented by a CAPES scholarship from the Brazilian government.

I studied very hard to earn excellent grades. I needed to successfully complete my studies to fulfill my obligations and indebtedness to these individuals and organizations. There was no "free lunch." The money was given with the expectation that I would do well in my studies. And that is one of the things that has changed in this day and age—some students today expect scholarships without maintaining their grades for them. It is the negation of meritocracy and will cost us dearly in the future.

The fourth example of imagination at its best came about during my term as director of operations at Lilly Brazil. We were continually looking for great talent for the sales force and then in 1986, I realized we were leaving out 50 percent of the population—women. Extensive arguments with the national sales manager ensued. Little by little, by "Fighting the Good Fight," I convinced him it was the right thing to do despite it being an initiative that had never been tried before. There was risk and there were resulting disruptions, but through perseverance, we successfully added women to our sales force.

The fifth imagination at its best experience, "The Arena Goes Global," involved three things happening at the same time. In my new position as director of pharmaceutical marketing planning, I began working with multiple countries instead of just one; I became more involved with PhRMA, dealing with intellectual property rights, pricing, and regulatory affairs on a global basis; and I became interested in changing the policies sustaining intellectual property rights in order to benefit the company. A few policy changes I supported and helped work toward included the recognition of patents in China in 1993, the World Trade Organization in 1995, and TRIPS—the pharmaceutical patent agreement. The triumph of going global led to disruptions that had to be managed in order for us to survive and prosper. A resilient industry emerged, and we ended in a better place than before.

The sixth example of imagination at its best revolved around "Doing Well by Doing Good." The Market Access Initiative which I was chairing eventually proposed making anti-retroviral products available to developing countries at $1.50 to $2.00 per day of therapy instead of the typical $30 per day. Through the help of several NGOs, we turned the initiative into a major success despite some disruptions along the way.

The seventh and final example of imagination at its best took place during "The Academy at Last." Of my many responsibilities as dean of WVU and chancellor of UNCW, I fought hard for the defense of free speech, particularly during my time at UNCW. Free speech is fundamental to a university. What amazed me was that many of the faculty, with all their knowledge and expertise, seemed oblivious to what was happening and were willing to sacrifice freedom of speech for the politics of the day.

I should thank our Board of Trustees, Board of Governors, the presidents of the Board of Governors, and the president of the UNC system for the support they provided for the defense of free speech. Other boards might have "caved in," but these men and women never did. We preserved the nature of the First Amendment. The triumph of free speech allowed the universities to press on without compromising such a fundamental right.

9

REFLECTIONS AND OBSERVATIONS

While reflecting on the jobs I have held over the past forty-nine years and the critical managerial functions those positions required, I extrapolated the following comparisons between corporate and academic work. Each field offered pros and cons, which made my career both exciting and challenging.

OBSERVATION #1 - VISION / MISSION

Both corporate and academia are very good at articulating their mission and vision.

OBSERVATION #2 - STRATEGIC PLANNING

Strategic planning is pursued with more rigor in corporate than in academia, particularly concerning the identification of critical goals and metrics. As chancellor at UNCW, I was surprised when one of the professors suggested we were moving too fast, that a good strategic plan should take five years to prepare. I almost fell off my chair. That comment motivated me to finish the plan in nine to twelve months, which included twenty-five to thirty strategic goals.

In some of the corporate jobs I had (such as the president of Asia Pacific, Japan, Middle East, and Africa for Bristol-Myers Squibb), we had to create a diverse plan that addressed the entire region. Then, more than fifty affiliates prepared their own strategic plans that complemented the regional operating plan. It was critical to create clear and succinct guidelines for everyone. At UNCW, I made sure our university-wide strategic plan was extended to colleges and schools and in some cases, to a few functional areas, too, such as IT.

OBSERVATION #3 - MASTER PLANNING

Master planning in corporate and in academia is something that takes considerable amounts of time but serves as a good road map for the physical nature of the institutions. In general, I believe academia does this fairly well. It gathers the information carefully and typically seeks the advice of consultants.

One of the things that bothered me at the university was that some recommendations required approval from the state legislature in order to get funding. This often resulted in delays as we lobbied beyond the academic school year. At UNCW, for example, it took us three to four years of continuous lobbying to get the library expansion project approved. In corporate, as soon as we were able to show that the expected returns were greater than the cost of the project, we were immediately granted the money to fund it.

OBSERVATION #4 - BUDGETING

Both corporate and academia budget very well, thanks to the critical guidelines provided by the system or home offices. Both corporate and academia put out profit-and-loss statements, balance sheets, and cash flows. These three reports are connected, and it is imperative that corporate professionals and academic staff/faculty understand them and consider their implications for the business/institution.

The budgeting for corporate and academia follow different standards, however. Corporate follows the Financial Accounting Standards Board and the standards set by Generally Accepted Accounting Principles (GAAP), which are used by all public companies and nonprofits. The Government Accounting Standards Board is followed by state and local governments and although different, they also follow GAAP.

In contrast, academia follows state guidelines that restrict how certain monies can be spent (although I suspect this is different for private universities). Tuition, for example, cannot be used to support athletics.

OBSERVATION #5 - SALES / ENROLLMENT

Sales and enrollment forecasting are done well by both corporate and academia. Large global companies with multiple-country operations require a precise set of expectations since our numbers forecasting could affect the guidance provided to the stock market and the Securities and Exchange Commission. Accurate projections are critical for fiduciary responsibility.

The projections in academia are softer and fewer people seem to be committed to achieving the goals.

OBSERVATION #6 - SUCCESSION PLANNING

Succession planning in corporate is expected and done all over the world. General managers and high-level supervisors are required to discover and prepare his or her replacement. If this isn't done, it results in a "ding" against his or her performance.

In academia, I soon realized that succession planning at any level simply is not done. In fact, the boards and HR departments had never even considered it. Instead, they rely on outside talent—a nationwide army of underpaid faculty and staff willing to leave one institution for another in the hopes of a better salary.

OBSERVATION #7 - SENSE OF BELONGING

At the corporate level, particularly within the companies I worked for, people jump over hoops to work there. Once they are hired, retention is high and the executives do everything they can to prolong their stay. I suspect the same occurs at flagship universities (R1-Doctoral Universities) because of how competitive it is to enter them.

At the undergraduate college level, however, it's a challenge to convert lukewarm students into highly motivated and dedicated students. Academia has to find ways to change this, which I believe starts with first-year retention and extends to other actions that impress a sense of belonging. When a recent study showed a correlation between a student's sense of belonging and high performance and that the sense of belonging differed dramatically between the various races, UNCW's Academic Affairs and Student Affairs began brainstorming ways to change the disparities.

OBSERVATION #8 - DIVERSITY, EQUITY, AND INCLUSION

Neither corporate nor academia have done a super job with this. Both have done a lot for diversity, but not nearly enough time and effort have been applied toward inclusion, let alone equity. At institutions of higher learning, improving communication and representation are particularly needed at the undergraduate level.

Upon my arrival at UNCW in 2015, we assigned a professional to specifically address this area. When the social justice movement exploded in the summer of 2020, the professional resigned from his position and we had to start all over again. But when the African American students provided us with a list of their needs, that finally started us on a much richer path that I think will pay off in the future.

In corporate, the efforts toward diversity, equity, and inclusion are the responsibility of each individual operation, causing them to vary according to the demands of the region. So in countries like Australia and Brazil, we saw a lot of improvement, particularly on the diversity side. At corporate headquarters, I became involved with affinity groups relevant to our region, which at the time were Asian and Hispanic, and advanced the cause that way.

OBSERVATION #9 - RESEARCH AND DEVELOPMENT

The companies I worked for all invested heavily in research and development, each spending billions of dollars per year on both discovery research and applied research (different phases of clinical trials).

Once UNCW became classified as an R2-Doctoral University, High Research Activity in 2022, we spent more than $15 million on research and development, mostly of the discovery kind. Our objectives were to develop more PhD programs and focus on the right areas of research.

Each year, a ceremony at UNCW celebrated the professors who had been awarded grants for their research proposals, and another ceremony was for students to display their posters on the work they accomplished under the guidance of UNCW professors. Legislators, interested in attracting revenues to state industries such as food production or fisheries, were given tours of the research labs, as were the Board of Trustees and Board of Governors, who enjoyed speaking to professors and students about their research. The university's PR department produced publications and social media content that focused on these projects, building public awareness of the exciting research happening on campus.

OBSERVATION #10 - GOVERNMENT RELATIONS

In business, it is necessary to narrow down what policies to support. In the case of J&J, since we had three different product lines (pharmaceuticals, medical devices, and consumer items) we had to focus on intellectual property rights, pricing, and regulatory affairs. Intellectual property rights because we were in the innovation business, pricing because the costs of pharmaceuticals in many countries were government controlled, and regulatory affairs because our pharmaceuticals and medical devices required regulatory approvals to be sold.

UNCW, a public institution, is dependent on the state legislature for annual appropriation related to enrollment growth, special appropriations like the help we got during Hurricane Florence, monies for facilities, and funding for salary increases. The federal government did not provide direct monies except during the pandemic, when they supported us with $57 million dollars. All in all, I can say that UNCW's interactions with the government were successful. We always knew what we were pursuing and most of the time, got the results we wanted.

OBSERVATION #11 - LEGAL AFFAIRS

Corporate legal focuses on contracts and lawsuits, both from private parties and from the government. At the university, we also dealt with contracts and lawsuits, as well as special responsibilities regarding laws issued by the U.S. Federal Department of Education such as Title IX, which was passed in 1972 to protect against discrimination based on sex. Our legal department was helped by the attorney general of the state, who provided us with invaluable support.

In a litigious society, the vice-chancellor for legal affairs at UNCW and all the corporate lawyers in the three global companies I worked for were vital team members who supported me in my roles. They were without exception experienced, competent, calm, and resourceful.

OBSERVATION #12 - COMMUNICATION AND MARKETING

In corporate, I witnessed firsthand the crucial importance of having an extensive communication and marketing team. Additionally, global operations brought the challenge of communicating concepts across countries with different societal norms. It was necessary to identify critical customer groups on which to target our efforts.

At UNCW, that identification also took place, but the targets became more varied and complex: students, staff, faculty, politicians, traditional media, social media, influencers, alumni, government officials, NGOs, trollers, and so forth.

At the end of the day, both corporate and academia have to precisely target customers and effectively engage with them 24/7.

OBSERVATION #13 - TENURE

Tenure as such does not exist in the corporate environment, but it is a way of life at universities. Many universities have professorial review processes in place and my impression is that they have worked well. Tenure serves to protect the freedom of expression by faculty, which I think is important.

However, I think it should be modified to include continued reviews. The current process is that once a faculty member becomes tenured as an assistant professor, he or she must be reviewed again before being promoted to associate and again before being awarded full professorship. After that, reviews stop. I believe reviews should continue every five years to ensure continued performance and productivity.

OBSERVATION #14 - SHARED GOVERNANCE

Shared governance does not exist in the corporate world, but it is understood that a successful executive brings staff and coworkers into the decision-making process anyway.

At the university, it is necessary to do the same with its plethora of constituents (faculty, staff, and students). As chancellor, I met with the presidents of the Faculty Senate, Staff Senate, and Student Government at least once a month to get their opinions and feedback. In addition, I was in regular communication with a host of various groups and individuals ranging from provosts and deans to the athletic director and campus police chief. But ultimately, the final decision rested with me (and the approval of the Board of Trustees and Board of Governors for large decisions) since I was fiducially responsible for the institution.

A successful leader in academia learns to rely on all their constituents, listen to what they say, and then make a decision that will advance the growth and viability of the university and best serve its students.

10

MENTORS

The people who helped give flight to my imagination—my mentors—were a wonderfully diverse group of individuals. Twelve people in total, they included six women and six men. Four were Brazilian and eight were American. I trusted each of them implicitly, and they trusted me.

These individuals stayed with me for long periods of time at various stages of my life, offering direction and advice. Each of them encouraged me, challenged me, and boosted my confidence. A few invested in my education, some opened doors for my career, and others supported my decision to enter academia.

Following are the twelve valued members of the "village" who made my success possible.

Alzira Ramos dos Santos Sartarelli
Loving Mother, Risk Taker

My mother, Alzira, was born on a farm in the municipality of Ribeirão Bonito in 1915. Her parents were Luciana Lopez, a direct descendant of Portuguese immigrants, and Benedito Ramos dos Santos, a Brazilian citizen whose genealogy showed the diversity of the country— white, black, and maybe some indigenous ancestors. She had two brothers, Benedito and Francisco, and two sisters, Lazara and Maria. All of them remained close throughout their lives.

Despite a very rudimentary education and eventually losing eyesight in her left eye, she successfully raised six children, managed the house on the farm and in the city, and later ran the commercial venture that Carlito purchased in 1960. She made needed household products from natural ingredients while living on the farm, cooking on a woodstove without electricity or running water, and keeping an immaculately clean home. She cut and sewed her own clothes and those of her children and later in life made extra money by doing sewing repairs for people in town.

She was a lady with strong religious convictions and a natural resiliency, and she worked hard to keep the family together. She recognized the importance of family, especially after the deaths of her parents in the 1930s and 1940s and the unexpected losses of her daughter Isaura and her family in 1970 and her husband João in 1977.

One of the most remarkable things I had the chance to witness occurred when I won the AFS scholarship to come to America to finish high school. When I told her the good news, she teared up and gave a wise, honest, and supportive response: "I know this is going to be very tough on all of us—particularly on me. I will cry every day for a full year. But you have to go. Years from now I will be gone and you will need to fend for yourself. This is going to help you immensely." Wow! What a lady!

Many years later, Kathy and I brought her to the U.S.—she loved it! A few months after her visit, she was diagnosed with oral cancer that eventually killed her on August 16, 1992. Fifteen years after losing my father, I lost my mother, my guiding light.

José Sergio Laureano
Resilient, Loyal

Sergio was one of my best friends in primary and middle school, and we remained close while I attended Getulio Vargas. We spent a lot of time together in our childhood and watched many Westerns while he worked as a projectionist at the Cine Piratininga in Ribeirão Bonito. Our friendship and the ambience of the time (the early 1960s) remind me of *Cinema Paradiso*, the great movie by Giuseppe Tornatore.

We continued to keep in touch while I worked for three different global companies and he worked in São Paulo for Banco Bandeirantes, one of the major financial institutions in Brazil, between the 1970s and 1990s. He spent almost thirty years working five days a week away from his family while Maria handled the household and children. This sacrifice of separation was done so that he could send all three of their daughters to college. Each of them successfully obtained their college degrees and now work in the field of education.

Now, in his retirement, Sergio studies art and history. He and his wife, Maria, visited Kathy and me several times in New Jersey, West Virginia, and North Carolina, including the installation ceremony when I was appointed chancellor of UNCW in 2016. During several of their trips, we took them to visit the only Leonardo da Vinci painting in the Americas—the *Ginevra de' Benci*—at the National Gallery in Washington, D.C. When Kathy and I visit Ribeirão Bonito, they equally welcome us to their home.

Our friendship is one of those rare ones that despite not being able to see each other for months or even years, we can immediately pick up where we left off, even completing each other's sentences. Sergio exemplifies resilience and is a friend I can always rely on.

Janice and Lonnie Bell
Unconditional Supporters, Out-of-the-Box Thinkers

Janice and Lonnie Bell were my American "parents" during my one-year AFS experience in Dimmitt, Texas (1967–1968). They were very interested in expanding their worldview since they lived in a small town. However, Lonnie had traveled far from home during the Korean War and maintained a library in their basement consisting of hundreds of books on the Holy Land and religion.

Lonnie had a good-natured sense of humor that surprised me time and time again. Janice held the position of president of AFS in Dimmitt and led the way for the Bell family to host a second AFS student from New Zealand in the 1970s.

They provided me with many unforgettable experiences. Sunday pot-roast dinners. Participation in their Church of Christ activities. Spending time with Lonnie's mother, Polly, who had witnessed more than a century of Texas history (she died at the age of 102). Riding along the farm roads in Lonnie's pickup truck, his head turned out the side window to check on the fields while he drove with one hand on the wheel.

Lonnie and Janice were loving, supportive people who helped me far beyond my one year of high school in Texas. Lonnie connected me with one of his acquaintances living in Brazil, which led me to become an English teacher in São Paulo. And together, they served as advisors as I began to navigate corporate life.

The Bells were two angels who happened to get interested in me when I applied to the AFS program. They inspired me, provided direction, and never gave up on their "son," even though he might be living ten thousand miles away in Singapore. I am eternally thankful to them for making that life-changing AFS experience possible for me.

Dona Deoclecia do Prado Bento and Dr. Antonio Monteiro Machado
Angels of Mercy

In 1969, I was able to become an English language instructor at the LICYLL. It was there I had the chance to meet Dona Deo, who was one of my students in the afternoon classes. After a few months, she requested private classes, and I taught her at her and her husband's apartment in the Perdizes neighborhood.

As 1969 drew to a close, I became more interested in business than engineering, and in December, I took the test to be considered for PUC (the Pontifical Catholic University) and the Getulio Vargas Foundation/São Paulo School of Business Administration (FGV/EAESP). I was accepted into both, which made for a difficult decision.

Dona Deo was proud of my acceptance to Getulio Vargas, which was the best in the country, and encouraged me to select that school. When she learned I couldn't afford FGV, she spoke with her husband, Dr. Antonio, and they agreed to provide me with the income from one of their rental income properties to pay for my studies.

Wow! How did I find such wonderful people to help me? Was it really happening or was I dreaming? Without knowing me well, Dona Deo and Dr. Antonio were willing to give an incredibly generous gift.

I am eternally thankful to them for what they did. They were like angels of mercy who showed up at the right time and did a great deed.

Dr. Donald A. Taylor
Internationalist, Link to Michigan State

I met Dr. Taylor, a professor at Michigan State University, in early 1974 while serving as his translator at a lecture series for business executives at the Getulio Vargas Foundation in São Paulo. I had the chance to spend more time with him afterward and shared that I had applied to earn an MBA at Michigan State.

When I began to receive acceptance letters from other schools but heard nothing from MSU, I reached out to Dr. Taylor. I informed him that if MSU did not act quickly, I was going to go to another Big Ten school. In a couple of days, I received an acceptance from MSU.

Don was a Canadian war hero—a navy man who had crossed the Atlantic fourteen times carrying troops, including the first wave of troops to land on Omaha Beach in Normandy on D-Day. In addition, Don had been a leading voice in the creation and development of the Getulio Vargas Foundation in São Paulo. A discussion about his work in this area can be found in the book *Institution Building in Business Administration* published by the school in 1968.

After I earned my MBA at Michigan State, I opted to stay and earn a PhD as well. For my dissertation, I had to put together a four-member dissertation committee, one of whom would serve as a lead advisor. Over time the initial lead did not work well for me, so I asked Don to be my lead. He not only welcomed the opportunity but truly provided greater impetus to the process. When I received my PhD on December 12, 1979, there was not a question that Don's imprint was clearly there.

We maintained such a degree of mutual respect for each other that I invited Don to be my best man at my wedding on September

6, 1980, which he accepted. He and his wife, Shirley, joined us in Pittsburgh to wish us well. When he passed on April 14, 2006, I felt I had lost a great friend and supporter, a true internationalist, and wise counselor.

Roy Cage
Brainstormer, Shaper of External Environment

I first met Roy Cage while working as an Eli Lilly international marketing associate in Indianapolis. He invited me to join his task force, which was charged with restaging Lilly Brazil.

Roy and I hit it off quite well; he was creative, an out-of-the-box thinker, and a brainstormer who used his imagination quite aggressively to tackle any issues blocking success.

Not long after I joined the task force, he was named vice president for Eli Lilly Latin America, Asia Pacific, and Commonwealth Nations, causing our paths to diverge for many years. It wasn't until I took over as general manager and president of the Brazilian operation in 1988 that I once again reported directly to Roy. He was very supportive when we decided to hire women for the sales force and when we decided to offer a retirement plan for our employees in Brazil. He and I also worked together to build the incinerator in Cosmopolis, which illustrated the type of modern management and leadership we were engaged in.

Roy's many visits to Brazil and the brainstorming sessions we had with our managers set the tone for the conduct of our business in that country. By 1990, ten years after I joined the company, Lilly Brazil became profitable, coming in at #7 in the market (versus #22 in 1984).

He was instrumental in getting me started in shaping the external environment and encouraged every general manager to shape it, too. I truly became an international businessperson under Roy Cage's guidance, and for that I am eternally grateful.

Christine Poon
Visionary, Ethical Compass

As I transitioned to Johnson & Johnson in October 2001, I began working for Christine Poon for the second time when she named me a company group chair. My first experience with her was when she was president of Bristol-Myers Squibb International and I interviewed with her for a position at BMS, which I received in July 1997. I worked under her leadership for several years while at BMS and I was excited to work with her again at J&J.

Christine became a highly influential presence at both BMS and Johnson & Johnson. At J&J, she held the position of worldwide chairman of pharmaceuticals, which she grew to over $23 billion by the time she left in 2009, and served as vice chairman of J&J's Board of Directors.

She was a knowledgeable, ethical, and effective pharmaceutical executive, which were undoubtedly the reasons we hit it off so well. At BMS we shared the challenges of an international division fraught with difficulties and at Johnson & Johnson, we worked together to deal with the opportunities and challenges of growth and profitability at the highest levels.

Chris supported my group's efforts when we decided to sponsor the Beijing Olympics in 2008, and she supported the anti-retroviral initiative team I led that made our AIDS drugs available in the "global south."

Once she left J&J to become the dean of the Fisher School of Business at Ohio State University, she regularly encouraged me to become a dean, too. Eventually, with her nomination, I got the job at West Virginia University. Subsequently, she was one of the individuals who supported me as the next chancellor of the University of North Carolina Wilmington and was the guest speaker at my formal installation ceremony.

Chris and her husband, Michael, grew to become great friends. In 2003, Chris and Mike, together with two of her nephews, spent two days with Kathy and me climbing Mt. Fuji in Japan. What an experience! The four of us have also traveled together to other locations, sometimes along with other mutual friends such as Don and Mollie and Quinton and Jean to such destinations as Italy, England, and several U.S. national parks.

James Clements
Visionary, Empowerer

As I was preparing to join West Virginia University, I had the chance to meet with the President of WVU, James Clements. My first impression of him was that of a true leader: empowering, able to delegate effectively, and focused on a clear vision. During our conversation, he indicated he wanted a nontraditional leader, someone who could bring a "business mind" and a sense of entrepreneurship that did not exist at the business school at that time.

Once hired, I did not report to Dr. Clements but to Dr. Michele Wheatly, our provost. Nevertheless, his positive outlook on life and his trust in his employees permeated the university and created an atmosphere of achievement and success. He supported all my initiatives at the College of Business and Economics and was pleased with our team's management of the school.

I was honored when he appointed me chief global officer of the university before his departure, which gave me a greater perspective on the overall operations of the university. In addition, he also named me to the board of the West Virginia University Health Care System, which gave me a new perspective on the impact the university had on the entire state.

The three-and-a-half years I worked under his leadership served me well. By simply observing his behavior, I learned much that helped me at both WVU's College of Business and Economics and at UNCW.

Margaret Spellings
Champion of Students

*"All leaders are for a time. Times change,
and those times demand new leaders and new approaches."*

MARGARET SPELLINGS

Margaret joined the UNC Board of Governors on March 1, 2016, and just a few weeks later, she officiated my installment as chancellor of UNCW on March 31, 2016. In addition to providing me the freedom and support to be a great chancellor, she helped make many positive changes across the entire UNC system.

Her work included initiating a new strategic plan, keeping tuition the same, growing enrollment and graduation rates, and navigating the university system through the HB2 "bathroom bill" controversy. Margaret also explored the possibility of changing the funding process of the university system and allowed some chancellors, including me, to be part of the exercise.

She had a gift of hospitality, often inviting the UNC system Board of Governors and the chancellors for receptions at her home on Franklin Street in Chapel Hill. Her concern for the welfare of her staff and students was evident through her ongoing support of UNCW during Hurricane Florence, when she organized all the UNC schools to help us in our recovery efforts.

Her career across many fields has been inspirational to me as well. She served as the eighth United States Secretary of Education from 2005 to 2009 and went on to serve as president and CEO of the organization Texas 2036 and CEO of the Bipartisan Policy Center think tank in Washington, D.C.

She served as a great role model for me, setting an example of openness and transparency. I was fortunate to have worked with her during her three-year term with the UNC system.

Katherine Ann Sartarelli
Loving Partner, Family Life, Sounding Board

Kathy and I have been married for forty-three years. We met in August 1978 when she had just moved into Owen Hall at MSU as a graduate student in biophysics, and two years later, we were married. Since then, we have lived in many, many places. While working for the pharmaceutical companies, we lived in East Lansing, Michigan; Indianapolis, Indiana (twice); Caracas, Venezuela; Santiago, Chile; São Paulo, Brazil; Singapore; and Hopewell, New Jersey. During my years in academia, we moved to Morgantown, West Virginia and then Wilmington, North Carolina. Now, in our retirement, we live in Naples, Florida.

At each of these locations, Kathy supported the community through her volunteer work. In Princeton, she organized summer concerts, led garden club activities, and gave museum tours. In Morgantown, she joined the one-hundred-year-old Campus Club and in Wilmington, her involvements included the Friends of New Hanover County Library and the Cape Fear Garden Club.

Even though I maintained a busy work schedule, Kathy and I made sure to spend quality time together. In New Jersey, we spent the weekends in Princeton and reserved a place at the shore each summer. In West Virginia, we walked the rail trails and cheered on the Mountaineer football team each fall. In North Carolina, we rooted for all the UNCW teams ("Go, Seahawks!"), enjoyed wonderful a cappella concerts, and attended as many cultural and music events as possible on campus.

Kathy is an internationalist at heart, shares my love of traveling (see her following reflections about our trips to various national parks), has made many friends all over the world, and has provided me with the inspiration to "dare to soar," as is said at UNCW. In addition, she has been a steady presence in all the major decisions we have had to make, created welcoming homes filled with mementos of our travels and families, and helped us build an incredible circle of friends.

Kathy's love, inspiration, and connections have made her an indispensable partner in my "giving flight to imagination" journey.

HIKING THE NATIONAL PARKS: BEING INSPIRED BY NATURE

By Kathy Sartarelli

A triptych of Shiprock, a sacred Navajo site in Arizona.

Shortly before Zito began his position as chancellor at UNCW, we traveled to New Mexico and stopped at a restaurant in Abijou on the way to visit the Georgia O'Keeffe site nearby. Artwork by local artists covered the walls of the restaurant and we purchased the above triptych of Shiprock, the sacred Navajo site, in Four Corners County. Although student art was displayed on the walls throughout the chancellor's suite in Alderman Hall, Zito hung this image inside his new office. Today it hangs in the entryway in our home in Florida.

Being outdoors in open spaces, sitting under the shade of a tree, and hiking a trail to a stunning view has always been important to Zito. Perhaps it stems from his childhood, when he was surrounded by abundant flora and fauna in a semitropical forest in Brazil. Regardless, he has always looked forward to our national parks trips during our annual home leaves while living abroad. Each year we chose a different national park to visit.

Soon after we were married, my sister Susie, who lived in California, took us on the first of many trips together to the national parks. We rode in her green BMW convertible up switchbacks to Yosemite where we took a day hike along the scenic trails, ate a picnic lunch beside the Merced River, and viewed the majestic waterfall. Zito was always in the lead, letting us know if that particular trail was a good one based on the view at the end. Over the years we stayed at lodges in such national parks as Glacier, Kings Canyon, Mesa Verde, and the Grand Canyon's South Rim. We returned to our favorites several times; Grand Teton National Park and the Jackson Lake Lodge soon became the places we chose to celebrate important birthdays.

Zito reads Western history and admires the explorers, photographers, and businesspeople who imagined the parks into existence—as well as the National Park Service rangers, employees, and volunteers who continue to make the park experiences so special. We enjoy listening to the park-ranger talks at night, whether they're held indoors or out in the amphitheaters, and we often go on ranger-led hikes.

Bryce Canyon Trail, Utah. L–R: Michael Tweedle, Christine Poon, me, and Zito.

Zito and I take a chilly hike up Pikes Peak, Colorado.

MENTORS 255

Zito and I enjoy a beautiful sunset at Monument Valley, Arizona.

Zito stands beside John Wayne's cabin in *The Searchers*. Monument Valley, Arizona.

As a child, Zito enjoyed watching Westerns and other Hollywood movies in his small hometown of Ribeirão Bonito, where the movie theater was next door to his house and his best friend Sergio worked as projectionist and his sister Luzia sold the tickets. Thus, he was thrilled the first time we visited Monument Valley (a Navajo Tribal Park) and visited the building where *The Searchers* was filmed and saw firsthand the pillars and rock buttes that served as the background in so many of the Westerns.

The elements of landscape, isolation, perseverance, and the defeat of evil are still present in new Westerns and in reruns on television. One of our favorite Western stars was the decorated World War II veteran, Audie Murphy. During the pandemic, Zito and I found another favorite television show, *Hopalong Cassidy*—a sarcastic and strong character played by William Boyd.

A prevalent theme throughout Westerns is to show how to do the right thing. If there is one thing Zito left as a legacy in the business world, it was that he trained everyone connected with the mission to display independence, never leave someone behind if they ran into a problem on a trip, and never show disrespect or treat others with disdain.

In addition to hiking with Susie and her husband, John, we visit the national parks and sites in the Southwest with the same group of friends most years. This has been our tradition for so long that we are always thinking, *When can we go back to …?*

John and Susie, me and Zito at
Grand Teton National Park, Wyoming.

Zito leading the way at Bryce Canyon Trail, Utah.

EPILOGUE

> "Leadership, driven by imagination and complemented by excellence, is the formula for success."
>
> **JOSÉ V. SARTARELLI**

How can a person attain success when the future is made up of uncertainties and frequent changes? I believe success comes to those who can integrate leadership, imagination, and excellence at the same time.

LEADERSHIP

If one seeks the meaning of leadership, one will find all kinds of definitions. Let me give two examples. The first is from Dwight D. Eisenhower, a successful military leader and U.S. president (1953–1961): "The essence of leadership is to get others to do something because they think you want it done and because they know it is worthwhile…"[50]

---

50 *Remarks at the Republican Campaign Picnic at the president's Gettysburg farm, September 12, 1956.* Source: "Quotes," Dwight D. Eisenhower Museum website, https://www.eisenhowerlibrary.gov/eisenhowers/quotes#Leadership. Last accessed September 23, 2023.

The second comes from Lao-tzu, a famous Chinese philosopher of ancient times: "A leader is best when people barely know he exists. Not so good when people obey and acclaim him, worse when they despise him ... But of a good leader who talks little when his work is done, his aim fulfilled, they will say, 'we did it ourselves.'"[51]

Each of these examples can be effective, but I believe that leadership is exemplified by the courage to take on new things. In industry and academia, the ability to take action in a timely fashion and follow through to achieve a clear goal is something I believe leads to success.

Further, my understanding of leadership centers on two very practical things: the attributes exhibited by a leader and the values espoused by a leader. The attributes include:

- Envisioning/Imagining
- Passion/"Fire in the Belly"
- Interpersonal Skills
- Empathy
- Hard Work/IQ and EQ

When we work with people in an organization, we notice when these attributes are being exercised.

The values include a list I have shared with employees throughout my career and in a previous chapter of this book:

- Do not lie
- Do not bribe people
- Do not break ethical standards

---

51 Purportedly from the book *Tao Te Ching* by Lao-tzu (aka Laozi). Source: "Quiet Leadership: Achieving More through Humility and Silence," America's Small Business Network website, https://www.asbn.com/articles/quiet-leadership-achieving-more-through-humility-and-silence/. Last accessed September 23, 2023.

- Do not harass people
- Do not utilize funky accounting

I have found these five elements of ethics to be extremely important and useful in all areas of business and academia. They may seem obvious, but defining them and making them an expectation for your employees' behavior leaves no ambiguity and leads to fewer failures.

Yes, there is still bribery throughout the world, and unethical, inconsiderate treatment still occurs toward those who should be protected by law. Sadly, I have seen all these rules broken and careers ruined. But the best companies I worked for were able to inspire loyalty with high ethical standards at the highest level of leadership.

IMAGINATION

As I mentioned previously, everything I've done throughout my life has centered on imagination. Sometimes the imagination was driven by other people and I directly benefitted from it (like my brothers in "Tomatoes to the Rescue"), sometimes the imagination was my own, and sometimes it was a combination of the two.

Throughout this book I have identified several mentors who influenced my life. Several of them were visionaries and brainstormers. Their influence shaped the way I faced the world and sought solutions to problems and challenges. Sometimes the solution broke new ground, sometimes the solution required substantial conversations with lots of people, and sometimes the solution required a sole voice to rise above the crowd. The key is to stand on what you believe in and uphold your constitutional rights, not become politically compromised or unwilling to see different points of view. Open, unconstrained brainstorming is perhaps one of the best tools to encourage out-of-the-box thinking and unbarred imagination.

Thus, imagination can be exemplified by taking initiative and differentiating yourself from everyone else by doing something out of the ordinary.

EXCELLENCE

According to *Merriam-Webster's Dictionary*, excellence has to do with "the quality of being excellent" and "an excellent or valuable quality: virtue."[52] My definition of excellence is to get up on a Monday morning, go to work, and decide that you want to excel, not just be average or below average. It is to go to school and make sure you are fully committed to being the best, getting the best grades, writing the best essays, and putting in the best practice.

Being the best does not mean that you beat the competition, but that you beat the goals you set for yourself.

Clear-eyed leadership combined with "giving flight to imagination" at all times leads to out-of-the-box thinking. When you couple these new ideas with a desire to be excellent, they provide the "fire in the belly" that you need to succeed in business, academia, or any endeavor you pursue.

Excellence is exemplified by hard work and the desire to not only do the right things, but to also do them well.

---

52 Source: "Excellence," *Merriam-Webster* online, https://www.merriam-webster.com/dictionary/excellence. Last accessed September 23, 2023.

FAMILY

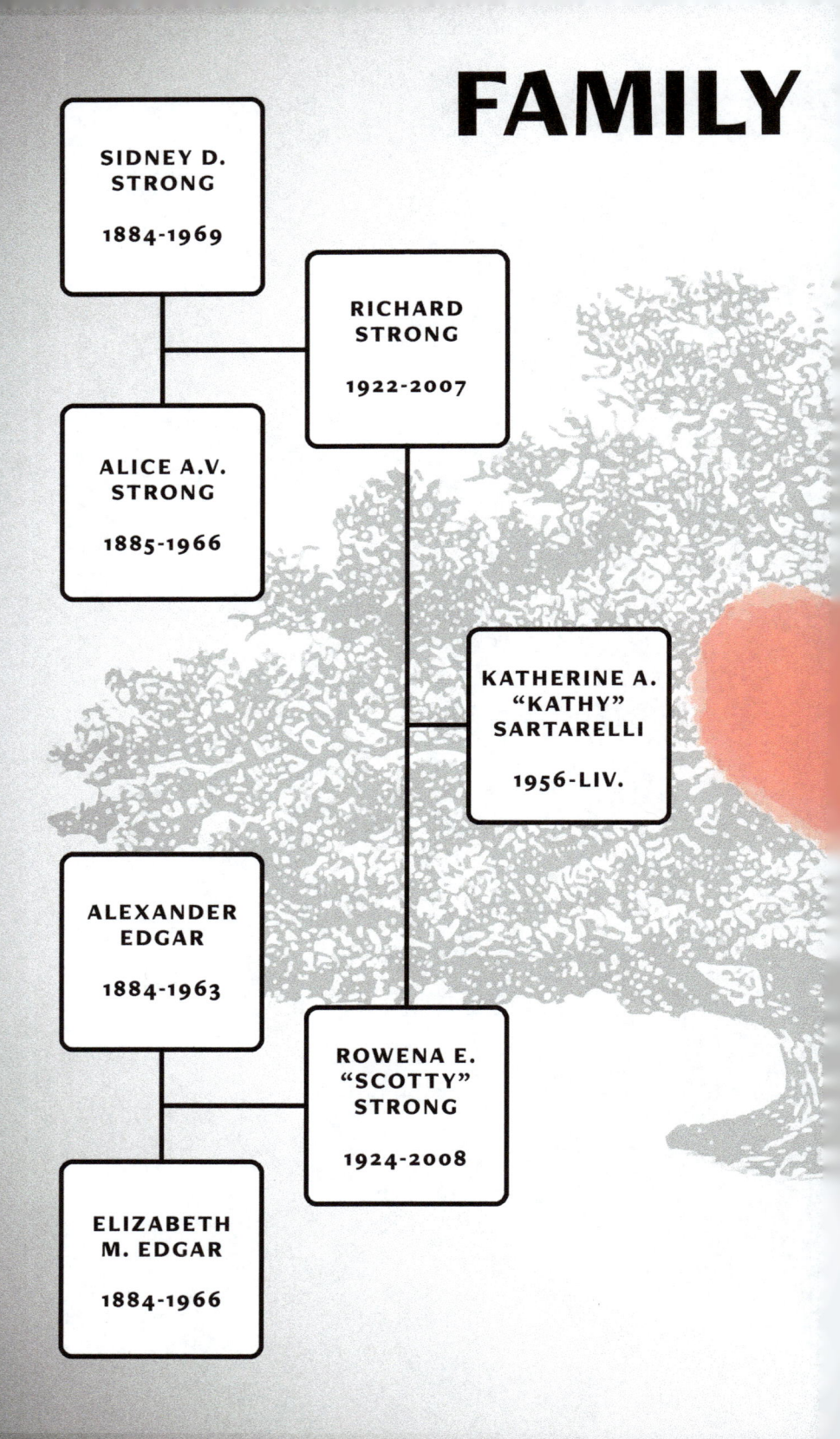

- **SIDNEY D. STRONG** 1884-1969
- **ALICE A.V. STRONG** 1885-1966
- **RICHARD STRONG** 1922-2007
- **KATHERINE A. "KATHY" SARTARELLI** 1956-LIV.
- **ALEXANDER EDGAR** 1884-1963
- **ELIZABETH M. EDGAR** 1884-1966
- **ROWENA E. "SCOTTY" STRONG** 1924-2008

TREE

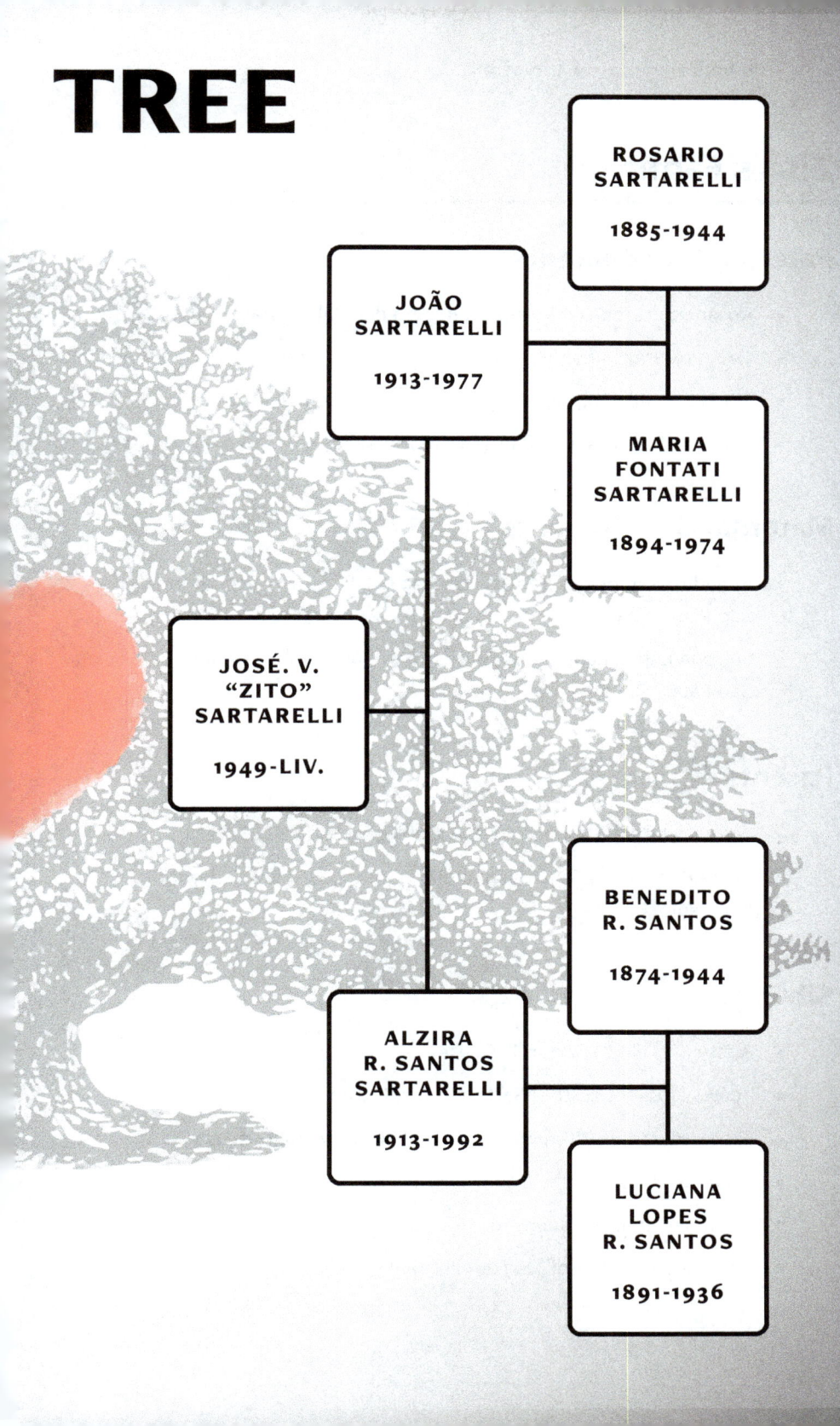

- **ROSARIO SARTARELLI**
  1885-1944

- **JOÃO SARTARELLI**
  1913-1977

- **MARIA FONTATI SARTARELLI**
  1894-1974

- **JOSÉ. V. "ZITO" SARTARELLI**
  1949-LIV.

- **BENEDITO R. SANTOS**
  1874-1944

- **ALZIRA R. SANTOS SARTARELLI**
  1913-1992

- **LUCIANA LOPES R. SANTOS**
  1891-1936

Zito's Family

Paternal Grandparents

- Rosario Sartarelli (1885–1944), Reggio di Calabria, Italy
- Came to Brazil at age 5 years
- Maria Fontati (1894–1974), Alta, Italy (near Padua and Venice)
- Came to Brazil as an infant (five months old)

Maternal Grandparents

- Benedito Ramos dos Santos (1874–1944), São José dos Campos, São Paulo, Brazil
- Luciana Lopez Ramos dos Santos (1891–1936), Ribeirão Bonito, São Paulo, Brazil

Parents

- Joáo Sartarelli (1913–1977), Dois Corregos, São Paulo, Brazil
- Alzira Ramos dos Santos Sartarelli (1918–1992), Ribeirão Bonito, São Paulo, Brazil

Siblings

- Aristeu ("Tilim") Sartarelli (1935–)
- Joáo Carlos ("Carlito") Sartarelli (1938–2010)
- Maria Aparecida ("Cidinha") Sartarelli Gomez (1940–2022)
- Isaura Sartarelli Rocha (1942–1970)
- Luzia Sartarelli Joaquim (1947–)
- José Valentim ("Zito") Sartarelli (1949–)

Notes by Kathy

Interestingly, there are not many people with the surname Sartarelli in Reggio di Calabria. On one occasion, Zito and I traveled there from Sicily across the Straits of Messina and hired a guide to look into church records; he discovered earthquakes had destroyed them. If we were able to find evidence of Zito's Italian ancestry, he could petition for an Italian passport, something that is frequently done in Brazil but which comes with some delay. In the meantime, Zito has taken it upon himself to become fluent in Italian; we spent a month in Italy in 2023 during which time he immersed himself in the language.

During one of our trips to Brazil, Zito, his sister Luzia, and I drove to where their paternal grandparents had lived in Dois Corregos. They resided in Ventania on a colonia (an agricultural village built within the larger plantation) where most of the other workers were also Italian. We then drove on to the nearby small town to visit the *cartorio* (notary public/records office) to document their grandfather Rosario's registration data.

Zito and his siblings have always enjoyed a close bond. Tilim and Carlito were the amateur country music duo, always ready and able to play all the classic Brazilian songs of this genre. For their careers, they transported workers to the nearby sugar mills and ran a provision bar in Ribeirão Bonito. Tilim married Maria Rosa and Carlito married Maria de Lourdes.

Cidinha married Clemente Gomez at a young age and lived primarily in São Carlos. For work, she did washing and housekeeping for her mother-in-law and helped manage a hotel with her husband for a time. She also helped raise her grandson in an effort to support her daughter's banking career, which frequently moved her from one city to the next.

Isaura was a sewing fiend and a very determined person. She married Darcy Rocha and lived in the town of Brotas. Unfortunately, her life—and that of her husband and one-year-old daughter Christiane—was cut short in a fatal car accident.

Luzia married Florisvaldo Joaquim and lived in São Paulo and São Carlos. She worked as a traveling schoolteacher, sent by the district to rural farms in São Paulo and São Carlos. Her husband was a great friend to Zito and me until he died.

All of Zito's siblings and their spouses were integral parts of every family occasion and celebration, and they often accompanied Zito and me on our excursions in Brazil. When we lived in Brazil, their children ranged in age from nine to eighteen, but they are now the parents of a new generation. We enjoy taking all three generations of family on trips with us around the U.S. when they are able to visit.

Kathy's Family

Paternal Grandparents

- Sidney Davis Strong (1884–1969), Plymouth, Michigan
- Alice Ann Vincent (1885–1966), Kalamazoo, Michigan

Maternal Grandparents

- Alexander Edgar (1884–1963), Kirkcudbright, Scotland
- Elizabeth McCutcheon (1884–1966), Springfield, Illinois

Alex Edgar came to the U.S. in 1906 in care of a shipment of cattle to Kansas. His father and Elizabeth's father were friends back in Scotland in their hometown, so he met Elizabeth in Springfield while visiting her family. She was born in the U.S., but Alex spoke with a heavy Scots accent. He only returned home twice to Scotland by ship for a visit, at the end of a successful career as the manager of the cattle barns at the University of Illinois. They lived in Williamsville, not far from Springfield.

All my father's relatives were from Michigan, so we often visited there while I was a child. I attended graduate school at Michigan State University and later, my sister Sarah attended MSU as well and still lives there today.

Parents

- Richard Strong (1922–2007), Plymouth, Michigan
- Rowena "Scotty" Elizabeth Edgar (1924–2008), Williamsville, Illinois

Siblings

- Susan Elizabeth Strong (1952–)
- Sarah Jean Strong (1961–)

My parents lived in Minnesota when my sisters and I were born and that was where we remained until we moved to Pittsburgh for my father's job at U.S. Steel. My sisters and I have always enjoyed close relationships with each other, and they were my bridesmaids for my wedding in Pittsburgh. Dr. Taylor and a friend from MSU were Zito's attendants.

Both my parents remained close to all their siblings, too. Vacations always revolved around visits with each other. We have old slides of aunts and uncles visiting us in Minnesota and of us visiting cousins in Connecticut. My father's brothers and sisters often treated my sisters and me to lunch when we were at university. Zito and I try to keep up that family tradition and even visit with cousins in Scotland as well.

My father was the family genealogist; he studied both Mom's and his family history. I have all his notebooks and photos from that work.

ABOUT THE AUTHOR

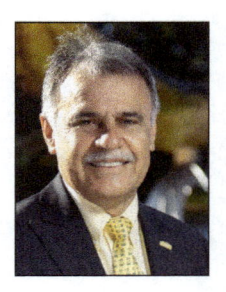

Dr. José V. Sartarelli is a champion of education, imagination, and free speech. After a successful thirty-year career in the pharmaceutical industry, he moved into academia, serving first as dean and then chancellor before retiring in June 2022. He and his wife, Kathy, currently reside in Naples, Florida.